D1342857

VOGUE

A–Z
of
WINE

ABCDEFGHIJKLM

First published 1984 by
Octopus Books Limited
59 Grosvenor Street
London W1

© 1984 text: The Condé Nast
Publications Limited
© 1984 illustrations: Octopus
Books Limited

ISBN 0 7064 1965 0

Produced by Mandarin
Publishers Limited
22a Westlands Road .
Quarry Bay
Hong Kong

Printed in Hong Kong

VOGUE

A-Z
of
WINE

Henry McNulty

Illustrations by Cherry Denman

Octopus Books

Introduction

The study of wines is fascinating. Every wine is a new experience because it is alive. Each bottle changes with age, with the way it is made, with temperature – in fact, its volatility is part of its charm.

Wine appreciation is a personal matter. Your own opinion about a wine is not to be challenged by any 'expert'. That it pleases you is all that is necessary. The fact that an expert considers it less than perfect should cause you no pain whatsoever, since appreciation is your own affair.

Having a few facts at your fingertips can help you to achieve a superior rank, a connoisseurship, and to enjoy wine even more. Providing easy-to-get-at facts for instant answers to questions about wine is the purpose of this pocket A-Z. It is also a personal approach to the subject.

People brought up in wine countries generally ignore rules about drinking wine. Tradition and mystery regarding wine help to add to its romance, but intrigue is one thing, enjoyment another. Real experts, a race with surprisingly few members, can tell what a wine is without recourse to label or price. They have a highly developed taste and a smell memory and a knowledge of how wine is made. A connoisseur (an easier category to achieve) can express his own preferences and tell which wine he likes and which he does not. A wine 'snob', on the other hand, is someone who drinks mainly by label and price, and emphasizes its faults instead of its virtues.

Being a wine snob is easy: hold your glass by its stem, swish the wine around in the glass, sniff it knowingly, think about it seriously for a moment. Make some profound remark about its colour or its smell or its flavour. The more outlandish your comparison the better.

Wine contains the Vitamin B you need for health and some of the mineral elements essential to human life. It helps to relax nerves and is an excellent tranquillizer. In reasonable quantities it makes you feel happy. A glamorous symbol of good living, well-being and civilization, wine is good for you. This guide is intended to help you to enjoy it.

AC (Appellation Contrôlée)

See French labelling regulations.

Acidity

Acidity is not just something to treat with Alka-Seltzer, it is one of the most important taste sensations in the flavour of wine. It helps to modify wine's natural sweetness, to bring a potentially syrupy wine to life and to give it bite. Without acidity, wine tastes flat; with too much, it can taste tart or sour. Acidity is also an essential component for ageing purposes.

If grapes get excess sun, they lack acidity and become overripe and too sweet. In cold climates it is the other way around; grapes do not ripen enough and need added sugar to cut the acidity. Cloying wines, that leave your mouth with an aftertaste of sweetness, have not enough acidity in them. The best sweet wines, however, like French Sauternes, German *Trockenbeerenauslese* or Hungarian Tokay, balance sweetness with just the right amount of acidity.

Africa, North

Algeria, Morocco and Tunisia are the three main wine-producing countries of North Africa. Most of their vineyards were originally planted by French settlers before the countries gained their independence. At one time Algeria was the fourth largest wine producer in the world. Most North African wines are fairly ordinary and are exported in bulk, though Algeria's best are excellent. Tunisia's top-quality wines are Coteaux de Carthage and Magon, both red, robust wines, and Haut Mornag, which can be red or pink. Morocco has modelled its production on French standards. Its red and rosé (*vin gris*) wines should be drunk young, but are very good. Its whites tend to maderize too quickly. All three countries control wine production fairly strictly. (See also Egypt.)

Age

Time, in the wine business, is money. Wines sitting in cellars, getting older and more luscious, are really dormant capital. That is one reason why top-quality wines cost so much.

Some wines *need* ageing. French Champagne, for instance, is not sold before it is at least three years old. It must be carefully stored in cool cellars until it is ready to drink. Other wines, like the finest red Bordeaux, may take ten to 30 years before reaching 'perfection'. Red Burgundy of the best quality generally needs about ten years to mature. Lesser French wines, like Châteauneuf-du-Pape and wines from the upper Rhône, can also repay keeping for up to ten years.

White wines, apart from sweet ones, need less ageing, but a great Sauternes or a Tokay will keep for decades. The best sweet German wines can last for a score of years. Fortified wines, like Port, Madeira and sweet Sherries, are usually sold when ready to drink. Italian Chianti and Spanish Rioja can stand seven to ten years of ageing. Good California reds, too, improve with age. (See also Storage.)

Alcohol

Luckily, all fruits will ferment naturally and eventually produce alcohol under the right conditions. Fermented apples are the material of Applejack and Calvados, fermented cherries of Kirsch, raspberries of Framboise and grapes of wine. It is the yeast enzyme in fruit that converts the fruit's sugar into alcohol.

Sweet grape juice becomes a sort of wine all by itself, even without human intervention. A grape's pulp naturally makes sugar as it ripens. It also makes acid. The balance between these two qualities depends on the amount of sunshine the grape receives during ripening. More sunshine gives more sugar, less sunshine produces more acid.

Grape skins have a whitish 'bloom' on them that contains

the yeast. They also have tannin, which helps ageing. When a grape is crushed lightly, it allows the yeast to work on the sugar and produce alcohol, plus a by-product that can be dangerous to inhale in enclosed cellars – carbon dioxide. The yeast feeds on the sugar until the alcohol gets to a strength (about 15 to 16 per cent by volume) at which the yeast can no longer function.

What remains is crude wine. Unless it is kept from contact with the air, this wine will turn sour and become *vin aigre* or vinegar. Wine-makers control this process to produce the wines we drink.

Most table wines have between 11 and 14 per cent of alcohol by volume.

Aligoté

Agreeably light, white Burgundy from Aligoté grapes. It is acid, dry and crisp. Wine snobs turn up their noses, but to my mind they underestimate it. When you are not trying to be high-hat, it makes a pleasant accompaniment to a snack lunch or to simply cooked fish.

Almadén

An important Californian winery. Its table wines are widely sold in the USA in carafes or jugs. Labelled by grape variety.

Aloxe-Corton

Among the best of fine Burgundy wine villages, famous for its *grand cru* vineyards on the hill of Corton. White Corton-Charlemagne (the red is called simply Corton) comes from the northernmost part of the Côte de Beaune vineyards. (Aloxe is pronounced *Alosse*.)

According to legend Emperor Charlemagne, a great wine lover, boasted a long beard. The original version (Corton) stained his beard red (a sure give away!). His wife, apparently not too understanding about his drinking habits, seeing that he had been at the bottle, would become difficult. To avoid this too-obvious sign that he had been enjoying himself, the Emperor commanded his vintner to produce a white wine to which he attached his own name. Presumably he lived happily ever after.

Alsace

One of France's smaller, but excellent, wine-producing areas near the German border, running parallel to the Rhine. Its wines are mainly white, fruity and drier than their German equivalents, but similar in style.

The countryside is deliciously French with German overtones (or vice versa!). Its villages are full of Hansel-and-Gretel cottages and the people are bilingual. Their wines are fragrant and quality is high. Alsace wines are called by varietal names of the grapes used – Riesling, Gewürztraminer, Sylvaner, Muscat, Pinot Gris (or Tokay), Pinot Blanc and Pinot Noir (which is pink or red) – and come in tall, slim, green bottles. One Alsatian wine, Clos Landelin, is named after an expatriated Irish saint and martyr!

Amontillado

Amber-coloured Sherry, similar to Montilla, with a dry, nutty flavour.

Anbaugebiet

German term for one of their officially demarcated quality wine-producing regions, whose names must appear on the label. The Anbaugebiete are: Ahr, Mosel-Saar-Ruwer, Mittelrhein, Rheingau, Nahe, Rheinhessen, Rheinpfalz (Palatinate in English), Hessische Bergstrasse, Württemberg, Baden, Franken (or Franconia in English).

Anjou

Mainly famed for rosé wines, this Loire area also produces a great deal of white wine and sparkling wine. Rosé d'Anjou is one of the top French pink wines, fruity and fresh. The best is Cabernet d'Anjou Rosé. The Coteaux du Layon (AC area), just south of Angers, includes the appellations of Quarts de Chaume, which produces a luscious white dessert wine, and the excellent Bonnezeaux. Nearer Angers is another lovely white wine called Savennières – best when well aged.

Appellation Contrôlée (AC)

See French labelling regulations.

Arbois

Agreeable light wines – red, white and rosé – from the French Jura mountains. I especially like the yellow *vin jaune*. Henry IV, King of France in the sixteenth century, tasted this molten-gold wine, smacked his lips and ordered more.

Argentina

Fifth biggest wine-producing country in the world. Most of its output is sold in South America. Some is quite good quality, including inexpensive whites, reds, 'sherry' and 'port' types.

Asti

An Italian region, around the town of the same name, just

south-west of the Alps, where one of the world's best-known sparkling wines – Asti Spumante – is made. It is light compared to French Champagne, with only around eight per cent of alcohol. Made mainly from Muscat grapes, it is inclined to be slightly sweet and rather 'grapy'. The best is made by the *méthode champenoise*, but the *cuve close*, or tank process, is also used. The sparkle is inclined to disappear faster than that of true Champagnes.

Auslese

The third rung of the QmP quality ladder of German wines. It means 'selected' in German, referring to the ripest selectively picked bunches of grapes that contain a maximum of natural sweetness. Auslese wines are sweet. (See also German labelling regulations.)

Ausone, Château

During the Roman occupation of Gaul the one-time consul and Latin poet Ausonius bought some vineyards in what today is Saint Émilion, east of Bordeaux. Château Ausone is said to stand on the foundations of his villa. His wine was the favourite of the Emperor Gratian. Today, after a period of some drop in quality, it once again merits the title *premier grand cru classé* of Saint Émilion. A small vineyard of seven hectares (17 acres) with a deep, rock-hewn cellar, Ausone is set apart as one of two 'first among firsts' of the region's 12 great growths. The other is Château Cheval Blanc.

Australia

A comparative newcomer to high-quality world wine production, although it has been making wine longer than California. Australia's wine output used to be consumed mainly 'down under', but its wines have recently made tremendous strides. Some can compete on even terms with their European and Californian counterparts. Varietal labelling is making them more identifiable as to type.

Its Hunter Valley wines in New South Wales are very good, as are some wines made in the states of South Australia, near Adelaide (particularly in the Barossa Valley), and Victoria, near Melbourne. New regions lie in Western

Australia, such as Margaret River, Mount Barker and the Swan Valley, near Perth.

The Aussies have been innovative about wine since they landed on the continent in 1788. Among their new ideas has been an attempt to find out which pigments or colour elements make wine red, yellow or white, through colour research by the Australian Wine Research Institute at Adelaide, and experiments with refrigeration and other modern scientific procedures that are making it possible to control the speed of fermentation. One of the country's top scientists, Professor John Fornachon, is trying to improve the 'flor' technique of making Sherry. Some experts believe that Australian wines, along with California's, will be among the world's best in another generation or so.

Australian vineyards enjoy almost perfect and predictable climatic conditions. They are dotted across the southern Australian landscape for some 3,000 kilometres (1,865 miles), but produce only one per cent of the world's total wines.

Australia also produces sparkling wines, dessert wines and brandy.

Austria

Austrian wines are made in the German style, some of the richer ones being comparable to the German in quality, but less expensive to buy and often of higher alcoholic strength. Some are lively, spicy wines; others are rich, luscious dessert types.

Most Austrian wines are white, light, crisp and fruity (40 per cent are made of Grüner Veltliner grapes). Its vineyard area lies in its eastern half around Vienna, along the Danube and south of it; and also farther south near the Yugoslav frontier.

Among the most agreeable drinking places in the world are outdoor cafés (called *heurigen*) in Vienna's Grinzing and other suburbs. Singers, actors, artists and just plain people are likely to gather in them on a summer evening. If they have imbibed enough, they are sure to burst into song!

One of Austria's biggest wine producers is the firm of Lenz Moser. They have a Malteser brand, named after a castle that belonged to the Knights of Malta, and claim it to be 'the Chablis of Austria'. There is also the unfortunately named 'Schluck', white and popular.

Bardolino

Light, good red Italian wine from Lake Garda.

Barolo

Soft, velvety wine with a brownish tinge and a violet
bouquet. Produced near Turin from Nebbiolo grapes, it is
one of Italy's best – dark, alcoholic, dry.

Beaujolais

Both a region of Burgundy just north of Lyon, and its wine.
The best of its wines come from a group of villages (some
40 of them) in the northern half of the area and classified as
Beaujolais Villages. Nine of these, the *grands crus*, usually
produce the best Beaujolais – excellent, agreeable wines.
These are Fleurie, Chiroubles, St Amour, Chénas, Juliénas,
Brouilly, Côte de Brouilly, Morgon and Moulin-à-Vent, and
are entitled to use their own names as appellations. Most
Beaujolais should be drunk young, but these nine (though
'why?' is a good question) can be kept for several years.

Beaujolais *Primeur* and Beaujolais *Nouveau* are made quickly,
with only four or five days of vinification. Beaujolais *Nouveau* is
supposedly not to be sold before 15th November each year,
while Beaujolais *Primeur* is held until 15th December before
sale (although I don't happen to like either one – they are
too acid and thin most years). Beaujolais *de l'année* is Nouveau
that has not been sold by springtime, and is supposed to be
drunk up by the time the next Primeur is due! Beaujolais
Supérieur merely indicates a higher alcohol level (over the
minimum of nine degrees) and often has sugar added to its
must to allow it to reach this strength.

Beaune

Town at the hub of the best Burgundy vineyard country and the name of its wine. On the third Sunday of November, wines from the Hospices de Beaune are auctioned off, giving an indication by the prices obtained of the quality of the new vintage and what it is going to cost you. The Hospices is a charitable hospital, founded 500 years ago to serve the poor of the community. Its fabulous income is founded on ownership of some of the richest vineyards of Burgundy, all of which have been left to the Hospices through gifts from grateful patrons.

Beerenauslese

The top but one quality category for German QmP wines. The grapes are picked super-selectively, grape by grape, to obtain only those that are ripest for crushing into juice. The result is a luscious dessert wine. (See also German labelling regulations.)

Bereich

A German term meaning a district within a wine-growing region, or Anbaugebiet.

Bergerac

Both red and dry white wine from the Dordogne, the home of Cyrano of the long nose. The reds used to be shipped to Bordeaux for mixing with Bordeaux reds, but this ceased when *appellation contrôlée* was introduced in France. The red is like a light Bordeaux.

Bernkastel

Famous Mosel wine town and its wine district, noted for Rieslings. The Bernkastel Doktor vineyard is its most famous vineyard.

Blanc de Blancs

An expression originally used for French Champagne, it

became a 'cult' name for any white wine made exclusively from white grapes, especially in less prestigious white wine areas. (Black grapes make white wines, too, if the pulp is separated immediately from the skins when crushed.)

Bodega

Spanish for warehouse or storage vault (particularly for Sherry). The Spanish store their wines in buildings above ground, unlike the French and Germans, who used to prefer cellars, and still do when they can afford them.

Books on wine

There are many excellent books on wine, and the following are some that I can recommend: Alexis Lichine's *Encyclopaedia of Wines and Spirits* and his *Guide to the Vineyards and Wines of France*; Cyril Ray's *Wines of Germany*; Hugh Johnson's *World Atlas of Wine*; Jancis Robinson's *The Wine Book*; André Simon's *Wines of the World*, ably adapted by Serena Sutcliffe; Jan Read's *Wines of Spain* and *Wines of Portugal*; Melville & Morgan's *Guide to California Wines*; Peter Quimmes' *Signet Book of American Wine*; David Peppercorn's *Bordeaux*; Anthony Hanson's *Burgundy*; Burton Anderson's *Vino, the Wines and Winemakers of Italy*, also Harry Yoxall's *The Wines of Burgundy*.

Bordeaux

Prestige, thy name is Bordeaux!, when it comes to French wine-producing regions. (Well, I am a Bordeaux fan but some people might choose Burgundy for this encomium.) Bordeaux produces a huge amount of top-quality, delicately balanced, almost 'feminine' wine, which the British call Claret.

The region makes both red and white wines. The sweet white wines are among the best of their type in the world. Some good, dry, white wine is now being produced in Bordeaux, catering for the modern preference for dryness.

The Bordeaux wine area surrounds the city of Bordeaux, and is divided by the rivers Garonne and Dordogne, which flow together to become the mighty Gironde. Water has a great moderating influence on the climate of all Bordeaux wine areas, with the two rivers inland and the Atlantic only a

few miles to the west. The region includes several great wine-producing areas:

Médoc is the most 'classic', at the mouth of the Gironde just before it empties into the Atlantic, with its vineyards on flat sand spits, and where even mere farmhouses are called châteaux. Both its red and white wines are the criteria for excellence throughout the world. Its best growing section is the Haut Médoc, some of whose wines are sold under their commune names as Margaux, Saint Julien, Pauillac, Saint Estèphe. More frequently, they are sold under château labels such as Lafite, Latour, Margaux, Mouton, Léoville-Las-Cases, Pichon Longueville, Cos d'Estournel, Palmer.

Médoc vines have to work hard to reach water in the gravelly soil, probing as far as four metres (12 feet) down. (Margaux's soil has the deepest bed of pebbles.) Often their vines live for 80 years. Old vines usually produce the best-quality wines, though quantity falls. The old Médocais used to say, 'If you are standing on pebbles and can see the river, or across it, you can't help but make good wine.'

Saint Émilion lies farther east along the banks of the Dordogne. Its wines can be drunk younger than those of the Médoc. Most do not last as long either, though the area's *premier grand cru* (first great growth) wines equal those of the Médoc for longevity, and two châteaux, Ausone and Cheval Blanc, are its equal for quality as well.

Pomerol is right next door to Saint Émilion and produces a velvety wine, full, long-lived and luscious. Its best is Château Pétrus, which, although Pomerol was not classified in 1855, could be a *premier cru*. (Alexis Lichine, in his

suggested new form of classification, puts it in the top class of *crus hors classé* with Lafite-Rothschild, Latour, Margaux, Mouton-Rothschild, Haut-Brion, Ausone and Cheval Blanc.)

Entre-deux-Mers (between two seas, because the rivers are still tidal at that point) is between the Dordogne and the Garonne, south of Saint Émilion. Its appellation covers only white wines, made mainly from Sauvignon Blanc. Recently these have been made light, fresh and dry in response to modern demand. After Bordeaux Blanc it is the second largest white wine appellation of the region; a good, inexpensive wine. Red wine made in the area can only be *appellation contrôlée* Bordeaux or Bordeaux Supérieur.

Graves covers a long strip of land south of Bordeaux and, confusingly, includes another appellation within itself, Sauternes. Known mainly for white wines, it does boast one of the top reds – Haut-Brion – and several lesser but still outstanding ones. Château Pape Clément is one of them, and is the only vineyard I know of whose vines have been personally tended by a pope.

Sauternes makes a great deal of ordinary sweet white wine, but some of its châteaux make an extraordinary version from grapes that have 'suffered' noble rot. Château d'Yquem is the most famous, but La Tour Blanche, Climens, Suduiraut, Rieussec, Coutet and others make lovely nectar too.

Other Bordeaux names you are likely to encounter:

Barsac is legally allowed to use the Sauternes appellation. This area claims Coutet and Climens as top-quality *premiers crus*, and boasts eight of the 13 *deuxièmes crus* Sauternes.

Blaye, opposite Médoc on the other side of the Gironde, produces light white and red wines of fairly ordinary quality but pleasant drinking.

Bourg, another right-bank Bordeaux, is almost a twin to Blaye, making reasonably priced red wine as well as white for everyday drinking. Its best-known château is de Barbe.

Fronsac, near Saint Émilion, produces red wine. The grapes are grown on steep hills by the Dordogne, where Charlemagne once had a castle. Red Côtes de Fronsac encloses the smaller and better Côtes Canon Fronsac. Fronsac wines are hearty, deep-coloured, soft wines of good value.

Cérons is an area composed of three small communes – Cérons, Illats and Podensac – within the larger Graves area, all calling their wine Graves when dry and Cérons when sweet. They are yellow-gold wines, much like Sauternes.

The whole region of Bordeaux was, for centuries, under English rule, which is one reason why the British are so fond of their Claret.

The Irish, too, were great Claret drinkers and in the eighteenth century used to take it, not with, but after, meals. The gentry were fond of sports like riding, duelling and drinking. Beauchamp Bagnal, one such, owned Dunckley House in County Cork. After a day's hunting, he would invite his friends to dinner, to which he would bring two loaded pistols. After dinner his footmen would carry in a keg of Claret, whereupon Bagnal would shoot out the bung. The other shot was reserved for any guest who failed to drink glass to glass with him! History neglects to state how many friends he lost in this way.

Bottle shapes

You can tell a good deal about a wine from the shape and colour of its bottle.

French wines usually come in four different shapes, unless they are in jugs or carafes. These are: an abrupt-shouldered bottle for Bordeaux, sloping shoulders for Burgundy, tall, thin bottles for Alsace, and heavier, thick-rimmed, deep-punted ones for Champagne. Red wines are usually in dark-green glass, white in clear or light-green.

Most good wines around the world use shapes similar to these to indicate at least something about the style of the wines they contain. Recently, popular wine, or *vin ordinaire*, is being sold in larger containers, up to 300 centilitres (about 5.2 UK pints), which require a rather squatter shape, such as a jug or a carafe.

Italian Chianti used to come in flasks with round bottoms, held upright by straw baskets around them. The cost of making these baskets has changed that. Now, the best Italian Chianti (Classico) usually comes in Bordeaux-shaped bottles, which are better for laying down. Some Italian wines, however, have fantasy bottles (Verdicchio, for instance, in a waisted bottle).

Germans use tall, thin bottles and, rarely, a flagon-shaped one used exclusively for Franconia wines. The tall ones come in green for Mosel and brown for Rhine wines.

Spanish bottles often have a fine wire mesh around them. This has no significance, and is mere decoration. Most

Spanish bottles are of the Bordeaux type.

In the USA jugs or carafes are very popular for table wines. Otherwise, like the Australians, they use modified French-style bottles. In Australia 'box wines' are popular for ordinary wine. South African white wines come in tall, thin, German-type bottles.

Bottle sizes

Sizes until recently have varied enormously, but the European Economic Community (EEC) is ruling that all bottles must be 75 cl or multiples thereof (except half bottles and quarter bottles of course). These are the legal sizes for the USA, Australia and South Africa already. Meantime, European wines (because many were bottled before the rules came in) can still be found in 70 cl or 73 cl bottles. Some, before EEC legislation forbade them, were even 68 cl, depending on what the vintner wanted to get away with. Eastern Europe goes its own way using various sizes.

Half bottles are available in many cases but, though useful if you do not want to drink a whole one, they cost proportionately more. In the case of Champagne, they are filled by decanting from full-sized bottles, and thus liable to lose their sparkle quickly.

Supposedly, the best size for maturing wine (because it allows the optimum balance between the amount of wine and the amount of air that can seep through the cork) is a magnum, the equivalent of 150 cl, or two bottles.

Champagne from France has a range of bottles all its own. It makes quarter bottles (about a glass and a half), half bottles and magnums. Then it goes wild with a Jeroboam (4 bottles), Rehoboam (6), Methuselah (8), Salmanazar (12), Balthazar (16), and the now very rare Nebuchadnezzar (20).

Big bottles do not necessarily mean their contents are less expensive than the usual single bottles. Check prices.

Bouquet

The scent of wine (also called its 'nose' or 'aroma'). It comes from chemical elements in the wine, and is variously described by tasters as resembling violets, raspberries, peaches and other smells that the wines seem to imitate.

Bourgueil

This worthy Loire red wine from Cabernet Franc grapes impinged first on my consciousness when I was an office-bound war correspondent in Paris in 1945. It was the house wine of a then well-known restaurant, Au Petit Riche, its *fin de siècle* nineteenth-century interior still filled with hungry Parisians eating very poorly because of the wartime shortages, but drinking well. I've had a soft spot for Bourgueil ever since. It is a light, aromatic, characterful beverage, to be drunk at cellar temperature.

Box wines

An Australian invention becoming popular in Europe and the USA for table wines. It involves a plastic bag in which wine is vacuum-sealed. The bag is then contained in a cardboard box. It is supplied with a tap which allows you to draw off wine a little at a time. The bag, because of the vacuum, collapses as the wine is consumed, thus preventing air from reaching it; in this way the wine is kept in good condition for several weeks. At first the wines so packaged were table wines of mediocre quality. Better boxed Bordeaux and Muscadet are now available.

Brunello di Montalcino

Ask a knowledgeable Italian which is his country's best wine and he is likely to say 'Brunello di Montalcino'. It is one of Italy's most prestigious products. The original was made by the Biondi Santi family 100 years ago or so. Brunello must age four years in wood by law and qualifies for *riserva* after five. A fine red wine, it is now carefully made by several producers, south of Siena, from a variety of Sangiovese Grosso grapes called Brunello. It is one of the DOCG Italian wines (see Italian labelling regulations).

Brut

A French term meaning very dry. It is mainly used for the driest of Champagnes with hardly any added sugar (although some even drier wines are now calling themselves *Sauvage*).

Bulgaria

There are vineyards all over Bulgaria, with 18 officially recognized sub-regions. Cabernet Sauvignon is the best red, Chardonnay is the top white, with a large variety of other European and indigenous grapes. Bulgaria exports huge quantities to Russia and its East European neighbours, but has a great potential in the West.

Bull's Blood

The English name for Egri Bikavér, a Hungarian red wine that is rather too full-blooded for my liking. It is however the best-known Hungarian red wine in the Western World.

Burgundy (or Bourgogne)

This is a full-bodied wine, both white and red, from Burgundy in eastern France, that can keep its quality through decades of ageing. It is capable of standing up to such strong foods as red meat and game. Fine Burgundy is produced in smaller amounts than fine Bordeaux (less than a tenth of the quantity) and needs more expertise in buying because prices for the best wines have become astronomic in recent years. I tend to associate it with cold weather because of its robustness. Perhaps the apogee of Burgundies is Romanée-Conti, a wine that can cost £1,000 a case and more.

A couple of years ago, I had the good luck to be invited by Mme Bise-Leroy, one of the Romanée-Conti's owners, to a simple farmhouse on her estate. She was bent on proving that her 1975 range of reds, a vintage that was generally very poor, did not deserve the harsh words of wine experts who had stated, when the wines were younger, that they would not last. We tried not only Romanée-Conti but La Tâche and Richebourg 1975 (also among the highest qualities of Burgundy) both before lunch and again with delicious roast beef. I found them all to have aged very well, and to hold up nobly to Mme Bise-Leroy's exacting standards.

Burgundy's Côte d'Or (a name that does not appear on labels) is where its great wines are made, although in small quantities. They tend to be gutsy, higher in alcohol than Bordeaux, slightly sweeter and usually shorter-lived.

Burgundy stretches out over a long 240 kilometres (150 miles) of France, from the isolated town of Chablis in the north to Mâcon in the south, via Beaune and Chagny, and on to Beaujolais. Unlike Bordeaux, where each château has only one owner, Burgundy vineyards are split up into many sometimes tiny, parcels, so a name like Gevrey-Chambertin can be owned by several people. These owners may make and sell the wines themselves or sell them to *négociants* or merchant vintners. Thus it is often better to buy from, and stick to, a *négociant* whose product you know and like than merely to go by the name of the wine.

Burgundy appellations in the Côte d'Or are complicated. Starting at the top are the *grands crus* and *premiers crus* of the Côte de Nuits and the Côte de Beaune (the two sections of the Côte d'Or) and then the straight commune wines. The first includes the towns or communes of Gevrey-Chambertin, Morey-St-Denis, Chambolle-Musigny, Vougeot, Vosne-Romanée. The second includes Aloxe-Corton, Puligny-Montrachet and Chassagne-Montrachet (mostly whites).

Down the scale in reputation (though still excellent wines) come Côtes de Beaune Villages and Côtes de Nuits Villages. Then Bourgogne Hautes Côtes de Beaune and Bourgogne Hautes Côtes de Nuits; plain *appellation contrôlée* Bourgogne; Bourgogne Aligoté, Bourgogne Passetoutgrain, and the most ordinary (though it does not sound so) Bourgogne Grand Ordinaire. Finally there is the basic Bourgogne Rouge and Blanc. (Whew!)

Bourgogne Passetoutgrain is an inexpensive, common wine, made from a blend of Gamay and at least one-third of Pinot Noir grapes – a fairly ordinary red.

Other appellations are simpler. Chablis (q.v.) in the north has four, in ascending order: Petit Chablis, Chablis, Chablis *premier cru*, Chablis *grand cru*. Farther south the basic appellations are: Côte Chalonnaise (covering Mercurey, Montagny, Givry and Rully), Mâcon, the famous Pouilly Fuissé with an AC of its own, and Beaujolais.

Buying wine

A cellar or cupboard for wine should be as common as a refrigerator is for food. You should buy and keep in it wines – preferably good wines – ready to serve, wines for everyday drinking and wines for laying down. Wines you want to serve to guests might make up a tenth of your cellar, the rest (apart from ageing ones) can be what the British call 'plonk' – inexpensive wines for daily drinking. The wines in your store should, of course, be ones that suit your own tastes. You can collect rare old wines as you might collect books, but be careful not to keep them so long that they lose all their *pazzaz* – although it is difficult to keep a really fine wine too long.

Buzbag

The lovely name (included only because I like it) for a Turkish red wine of fairly weak quality, but certainly of powerful character.

Cahors

A dark-red, 'black' wine from the south-west of France produced along the River Lot, and the name of the main town of the district. In the days when Britain ruled that part of France, the Black Prince decided the river would be more useful if it were navigable, and in the mid-fourteenth century commanded it to be so made for his military needs. Later it was used to ship the region's wines down to Bordeaux for blending with Claret (now forbidden by EEC rules). Today it has a good reputation of its own.

California

In the last quarter of a century California's wine industry has burgeoned. It makes millions of gallons of very drinkable table wines, and some of its smaller, experimental vintners are producing both red and white fine wines to rival the best in Europe. In the early days Californian wines were called by European regional names, much to the confusion of tasters. Today they are producing 'varietal' wines named after the grape from which they are made.

Important vineyard areas include the Napa Valley, Sonoma and the San Joaquin Valley (home of table wines). Napa and Sonoma make some of the best quality wines. Good Californian wine producers include: Schramsberg, Christian Brothers, Spring Mountain, Cuvaison, Louis Martini, Joseph Heitz, Robert Mondavi, Domaine Chandon, Sebastiani, Parducci and Mirassou.

In addition there are: the Russian River area, north and west from Santa Rosa (where Korbel, Parducci and Italian Swiss are important names); the areas along the Salinas River Valley, with Paul Masson and Almadén; Livermore, where Wente are the big producers, and the San Joaquin Valley, where Gallo is king and Franzia and Guild, too, produce large quantities of 'jug wine'. (See also Napa Valley, Sonoma, USA, New York State.)

Carbonnieux, Château

A château in the Graves area of Bordeaux. In François I's day, around 1520, the French ambassador to the Sultan at Constantinople decided to present a selection of Château

Carbonnieux to the teetotal Moslem prince. Not surprisingly, everyone thought he was mad. However, the wily ambassador labelled his gift *Eau Minérale de Carbonnieux* and brought it in as a special drinking water. The Sultan was delighted, but bewildered. 'How can you French drink wine,' he asked, 'when your mineral water is so good?'

Today the predominantly white wine is one of Graves' best.

Cellars

See Storage.

Chablis

The northernmost Burgundy wine area, the name of its main town and the wine made around it. Chablis *grands crus* are magisterial great wines that keep improving for some ten years. Chablis *premiers crus* are not quite as good, but still top-notch. All true Chablis are *appellation contrôlée*, crisp, light, dry and delicious.

Plenty of other wine-growing nations, including the USA, have tried to make Chablis, but they do not taste the same. Sniff a glass of the driest and best non-French 'chablis' you can find and compare it with a true, good French Chablis. Even a tyro taster can tell the difference.

Chai

French for a wine warehouse.

Chambertin

Grand cru vineyard in the commune of Gevrey-Chambertin and its wine. This famous Burgundy from the Côte d'Or was Napoleon's favourite wine. His orderly forgot to include it in his stores the day before Waterloo. Legend has it that lack of it upset the Emperor so much that he could not concentrate on the battle and lost it as a result.

The 'champs de Bertin', belonging to a local farmer, used to be part of the Clos de Bèze monastery. Shortening the name to Chambertin, its wine became far more renowned than its parent.

Champagne

By reluctant international agreement, the only sparkling wine allowed this appellation is the 'king of wines' from the French Champagne country east of Paris. Although it is predominantly a white wine, it is made, for the most part, from black grapes whose skins are held apart from their juice as soon as the grapes are pressed.

The *méthode champenoise* allows the wine to ferment a second time. It is bottled after yeast and sugar are added to the wine, which causes a second fermentation to take place. The bottles are stored horizontally in cellars for one to three years, the sediment remaining in the wine. The bottles are then stacked with their necks down in huge jiggling machines holding 100 bottles or so and looking like rows of rocket launchers. This jiggling job used to be done by hand, a much more colourful operation, with the bottles arrayed in wooden *pupitres*, but tending to give the jiggler (the *remueur*) the kind of heebie-jeebies Charlie Chaplin had in *Modern Times*. Today, most *remuage* is mechanical.

Once the sediment has been jiggled down onto the cork, the bottle necks are frozen. They are then quickly opened so that the carbon dioxide gas formed during the second fermentation in the bottle pushes the plug of sediment out. The bottles are then topped up, immediately recorked and fastened down with the familiar wire fastening, labelled and sent off to celebrate birthdays, New Year and weddings.

Champagne comes in varying degrees of dryness. The driest is *Brut*, followed by *Extra-dry*, *Sec* (which means dry, but isn't), *Demi-Sec* (a bit sweeter) and, rarely, *Doux* (sweet). The sweetness is adjusted by the addition of *liqueur d'expédition* before the final cork is inserted.

Many other countries can, and do, make sparkling wine, such as the Italian Asti Spumante, Spanish Cava and German Sekt, which are consumed like water. Actually, the only sparkling wine I know that truly compares with French Champagne is Chandon Brut, made in Napa by Moët et Chandon.

Champagne should usually be drunk by the time it is ten years old, although I have drunk one from the 1864 vintage, offered in honour of a venerable guest's birthday (not mine). It was still lively and sparkling 75 years later. But this bottle had lain in its maker's cellars, undisturbed, all that time. Charles Dickens called Champagne 'one of the elegant extras of life'. André Simon said: 'It is the best wine to drink in a garden.' In short, it suits all kinds of occasions.

Chaptalization

This is the practice of adding small, controlled amounts of sugar to fermenting grape must to raise the alcoholic strength of wines – not to wine itself. The process does not make the wine sweeter because the sugar turns to alcohol. It does change a wine's balance by increasing the alcohol, which makes the wine 'softer' and perhaps apparently sweeter.

Properly used it can achieve a balance between the acid and alcohol in a 'difficult' wine when the sugar content of the grapes is low owing to lack of sun during the ripening stage. Abused, it can allow a 'wine' to be made from skins, acid and sugar.

The process is used in Germany, mainly because of insufficient sunshine, but only for cheaper wines, not for QmP wines (q.v.). It is also used in a strictly limited way in Burgundy, for the same reason. It is not legal in southern Europe or California. It is allowed in very poor years in Bordeaux.

Chaptalization is hardly ever needed where the weather is sunny enough to ripen the grapes properly. The balance of a really good wine would be upset by chaptalization.

Château

Bordeaux wines, especially, tend to be called by château names. However, even in Bordeaux, there are literally

hundreds of châteaux which make as ordinary a wine as you could wish. Many would be called farmhouses in most countries. Some are so small they might even be called cottages.

Other wines of France, not to mention North Africa, and even a few in the USA, have taken château as part of their name. Some more recently established French wineries call themselves 'château' to add prestige to otherwise undistinguished reputations.

Lists of Bordeaux châteaux abound, but space forces me to give only a few names of some I happen to like: Ausone; Beychevelle, a real stately home if not a true château; Brane-Cantenac; Calon-Ségur; Cantemerle (a pretty name meaning 'lark's song'); Ducru-Beaucaillou; Gruaud-Larose; Haut-Brion, the oldest fine château of Bordeaux and only non-Médoc red wine included in the 1855 classification as a *premier cru*; Lascombes; Latour, most dependable of châteaux; Léoville-Las-Cases; Loudenne, a beautiful building with vineyards on its front lawn; Lynch-Bages; Margaux, a Greek Revival château; Mouton-Rothschild, with a fine wine museum; Pétrus; Pichon-Longueville-Baron; Prieuré-Lichine, belonging to Alexis Lichine, who improved it tremendously; La Tour Blanche, lovely Sauternes.sweetie; La Tour-du-Pin-Figeac; Yquem, the world's most famous sweet white wine and the one and only *grand premier cru* of Sauternes.

Châteauneuf-du-Pape

One of the best Rhône wines, Châteauneuf-du-Pape's 3,000 hectares (7,400 acres) of vineyard date from the days when the Popes moved their headquarters from Rome to Avignon in southern France. Its name comes from the then papal summer residence, situated on a cool hill just outside Avignon. It can be a robust, superb wine, strong in alcohol (13.5 per cent and more) and long-lived, though some of it is made for early drinking. Mainly red, its white is less known and inclined to be heavy.

Cheval Blanc, Château

Shares first place in Saint Émilion with Château Ausone; classified in 1969. The 1947 vintage was legendary.

Chianti

One of Italy's best wines, made mainly from Sangiovese grapes and produced in Tuscany between Florence and Siena. Ordinary Chianti used to be shipped in electric-light-bulb-shaped bottles with rounded bottoms that needed to be encased in straw for them to stand upright. Now the attractive straw has given way to plastic, but the wine itself has perhaps improved. It is lively and fruity at its best, light and pleasant drunk young, though its best will keep. One of the grapes Chianti is made from is the Canaiolo, or 'the grape the dogs prefer'!

Chianti Classico

This is the best of Chianti and one of Italy's top wines (soon to be upgraded to DOCG). It comes from central Tuscany with its capital at Greve. *Classico* means that the grapes come from the production heartland or the original Chianti area. Some 700 Chianti producers have formed a consortium that supervises quality and awards a Black Cockerel seal to those producers who stick to its self-imposed rules. It is an excellent, agreeably perfumed wine, aged in oak. *Riservas* (with at least three years of ageing) resemble Bordeaux, though with more body and less subtlety.

One *Classico* estate was founded by Machiavelli. Other names of note are Verrazzanno, Montepaldi, Serristori, Gabbiano and Uzzano. Not members of the consortium, but big producers, are Nozzole, Ruffino, Brolio, Antinori.

Classico's cockerel seal is based on a legend of the rivalry between Florence and Siena about their borders. It was decided to settle the argument by a race – each side would

send a knight to the other's territory. Where the two met would be the frontier. The wily Florentines used a cockerel as their alarm clock and got off to an early start. They met the Sienese at Fonterutoli, two-thirds of the way to Siena, and have practically bathed in Chianti ever since.

Chile

Chile, with only about six million inhabitants, makes half as much wine as does the USA. It has been producing wine, from European grape varieties, since the sixteenth century. It is South America's second largest wine producer after Argentina. Wine grape vines cover some 110,000 hectares (272,000 acres) and stretch for 1,500 kilometres (932 miles). Some good Chilean labels for both red and white wine are Concho y Toro, Cousiño-Macul, Undurraga, Canepa and Los Vascos.

Chinon

Pleasant, light, dry red wine from around the Loire town of the same name. Usually drunk cool, and young. Nice with a light summer meal.

Claret

A word used, mainly in Britain, for red Bordeaux wines. Henry II, who was French and ruled the French Atlantic coast as Count of Anjou, was also King of England in medieval times. He shipped light, red Bordeaux wines known as 'clairet' to England, where its pronunciation was altered to suit the natives. (See also Bordeaux.)

Climate

One of four factors that determine the character of a wine (the others being grape variety, soil and the wine-maker). The weather, especially in the most northern vineyards (or most southern in the southern hemisphere) decides the quality and quantity of the vintage: spring frost or bad weather at flowering will reduce the crop; lack of sunshine gives unripe grapes. The right amount of sun and rain can make a great vintage.

Clos

In most of France a *clos* means a mere farm enclosure. In Burgundy it is often the equivalent of a castle, as in Clos de Vougeot, with its 900-seat banqueting hall, its chapel and huge reputation. It is used to describe some of Burgundy's best vineyards, such as Clos Saint-Denis and Clos de Tart.

Condrieu

From the northern Rhône, where the capricious Viognier grape makes an unusual white wine, reminiscent of apricots.

Confrérie

There are a number of *confréries*, or brotherhoods, of French and other nations' wine lovers. The oldest and most prestigious is the *Confrérie des Chevaliers du Tastevin* founded (or perhaps 'revived' would be more like it) in 1933 to promote the good of the Burgundy region's wines. Members wear medieval-style robes and hand out diplomas to knowledgeable, or VIP, wine personalities from all over the world. New recruits are enjoined to speak often and well about Burgundy wine, and to behave likewise as to its use. The society holds numerous banquets, notably one at the time of the Hospices de Beaune wine auction.

Constantia

An important wine-producing region of South Africa. Also the name of a rich dessert wine popular in the nineteenth century from some of the oldest vineyards of South Africa's Cape, situated to the south of Capetown. Famous for 'Muscat' in its day, Groot Constantia is a beautiful, Dutch-style stately home. (See also Groot Constantia.)

Cooking with wine

One uses wine for cooking not because it inebriates, but because it adds flavour. Alcohol evaporates with cooking heat, but the flavour of a cup of wine added to a good stew improves and heightens the taste admirably.

Cork

Until about the end of the seventeenth century in Europe, bottles were stopped with rags or wax. The idea of using cork was developed in Spain during that period and reached France at the end of the century, then Germany and eventually England. Nevertheless, cork had been occasionally used before that by both the Greeks and the Romans. But they depended mainly on rags soaked in oil or on pitch. Cork began to be used more efficiently when Dom Pérignon found it would compress into a bottle neck.

Even today, most true cork comes from the Iberian Peninsula, the south of France and parts of North Africa. It is naturally compressible but not airtight, as well as being odourless, tasteless and reasonably cheap. Because cork is now used for other purposes, such as floor coverings and shoes, it has become dearer in recent years.

Cork comes from the inner bark of 20- to 30-year-old cork-oaks. It takes ten or 15 years to build up thickness, but once it is stripped off, the optimistic trees start growing a new bark layer.

For years the big French bottlers of *vins ordinaires*, like Nicolas, have used a combination of a metal cap over a small, reusable plastic stopper. This system works very well for wines for immediate consumption. Many bigger bottles (1.5 to 3 litres) are now also closed with metal caps. This does not affect the ordinary wine that most of them hold, because it is not kept for long.

Corkage

Corkage is what you pay to hotels or restaurants if they allow you to bring your own wine to drink.

Corkscrew

The invention of corks mothered the invention of the corkscrew. The best are the lever types used by most European wine-stewards, complete with bottle opener and a knife used for cutting the bottle-cap to leave the neck agreeably decorated with a ring of colour.

Buy only those with coiled spring-shaped screws. You should be able to thrust a skewer through the coil.

Corton

Home of some of the greatest red wines in the Côte de Beaune. If a label says Le Corton, or starts with the word Corton plus the name of a vineyard, the wine is *grand cru*, and a magnificently majestic, very expensive wine. It is produced in the commune of Aloxe-Corton. (The white wine is excellent, too.)

Corton-Charlemagne

After Charlemagne held off the Moors at Roncesvalles in AD 778, he donated 24 hectares (60 acres) of his rather extensive family property to provide funds to rebuild a church the Saracens had sacked. It was quite a present for, ever since, the wines produced on that land have been known as Charlemagne's wine and are among the best in France.

Corton-Charlemagne, a *grand cru* vineyard outside the village of Aloxe-Corton, produces one of Burgundy's great white wines, made from Chardonnay grapes. It is big and golden, rare and rich, steely and splendid.

Corvo

A strong, dark, dry red wine from Sicily and its soft, alcoholic white brother. Made outside Palermo, near some of Sicily's best Greek ruins, by the Duca de Salaparuta.

Côte d'Or

This is not a wine, but the name of the hillside on which the vines that produce most great Burgundies are grown. It is divided into the Côte de Beaune and Côte de Nuits.

Côte Rôtie

The 'roasted hill' of the northern Rhône, divided into the Côte Brune and the Côte Blonde. Local legend claims the vineyard was once owned by a man with two daughters, one a blonde, the other dark, between whom he divided his vines. The Syrah grape produces rich powerful wine from these sun-soaked terraced vineyards.

Crémant

A term for sparkling wines e.g. Crémant d'Alsace. In the Champagne area itself, *crémant* is used to describe semi-sparkling Champagne.

Cru

Translates as 'growth' in English. A *cru classé* is a classified growth, a term used in France, especially in Bordeaux, for vineyards that have been ranked. The lowest official ranking is *cru bourgeois*. Slightly better is the *cru bourgeois supérieur*. The leading *crus* are numbered up from fifth to second *cru* (cinquième, quatrième, troisième, deuxième). *Premier cru* indicates first or top quality in Bordeaux. Only four of them have existed since the 1855 classification. These are the châteaux of Lafite-Rothschild, Latour, Margaux and Haut-Brion. Château Mouton-Rothschild was decreed a first growth in 1973. The only *premier grand cru classé* (first great growth) on the right bank is Sauternes' Château d'Yquem. However, there are 12 of them in Saint Émilion and, although Pomerol has never been classified, Château Pétrus is considered to be the first great growth of the region.

Cuve close

A method of making ordinary bulk sparkling wine. Sugar and yeast are added to produce the 'second fermentation' in large tanks, rather than in bottle, and the resultant sediment is simply filtered out.

Cuvée

Usually a blend of wines, sometimes a special blend (*cuvée spéciale*). Also used in France to indicate a separate lot of a specific wine destined, perhaps, for a particular market.

Cyprus

The wines of Cyprus are similar to the wines of Greece. About 80 per cent are light whites and 20 per cent are heavier reds. Commandaria is a sweet dessert wine of quality. Main producers are Keo and Sodap.

Dão

One of the best red table wines from northern Portugal
(also whites), produced about 65 kilometres (40 miles)
south of Porto. (Pronounced *dow-ng*.)

Decanting

Pouring wine so as to separate it from any sediment in a
bottle, caused by perfectly natural ageing. Rarely is it
necessary to decant white wines and seldom, these days,
even most red ones. Fine Bordeaux or sometimes old
Burgundy, perhaps, should be decanted but mainly for
aesthetic reasons. Sediment in a glass looks unsightly and
makes a wine cloudy. The sediment itself does no harm, and
actually wine that is left from a decanted bottle can be kept
to cook with.

To decant a fine wine, stand the bottle on your sideboard
for a few hours before it is to be used to let the sediment
drop to the bottom. Then, an hour or so before eating,
working in front of a light, pour from the full bottle into a
decanter. The older the wine, the more sediment there is
likely to be. When only an inch or less of wine is left, or
when you see the sediment, stop pouring. Leave the
decanter open to let the wine breathe. After all this trouble,
because you should be proud of the wine you serve, leave
the empty bottle to show your guests (who will surely be
interested) what they are drinking.

Avoid using wine slings or baskets, unless you open old,
fine wines at home. In most cases, especially in restaurants,

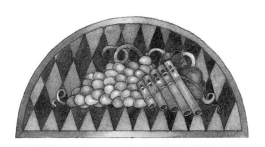

bottles have been whirled around from cellar to kitchen to your table, so a mere few minutes of lying down will do nothing for the sediment, if there is any. Also, the basket takes up too much room on an often crowded table. Don't wrap the bottle in a napkin when you pour it. As with the empty, decanted bottle, you should be happy to let your guests know what you are serving.

Decanting can marginally improve young wine by aerating it and letting it 'breathe'. Air helps to soften and 'age' young wines. With very old wines, however, air can destroy what little life is left in them.

Deidesheim

One of the picturesque wine villages of the Rheinpfalz (Palatinate) vineyard region, not far from Karlsruhe. Wine from the district is aromatic and low in acidity. Grapes used are mainly Müller-Thurgau, Sylvaner and Riesling.

Demestica

A table wine from Greece that goes well with kebabs and moussaka. In Greece it is ubiquitous and dependable, made by the country's biggest wine firm in its biggest wine-producing area, the Peloponnese.

Distributors

Discovery of a good wine merchant or shipper can be the best investment you make in buying wine for your home use. Most people in the wine trade know wines, or at least their own stock, and can give you advice about what and how to buy to your own needs and tastes. This is perhaps not so true of chain stores and department stores, but their buyers usually look for and sell wines that they have tasted and have considered to be good value for money. Wine clubs, such as Les Amis du Vin, usually have a good range of special wines, hold tastings and lectures, and charge a nominal membership fee, which implies that they will advise you if you need advice.

Whatever method of buying you use, it is wise to avoid too much hocus-pocus about prestige wines. There should be no more ritual about selecting a bottle of wine than

there is about a jar of jam. You should buy what you can afford (and attempt to find the best prices) but you should not buy on price alone. Sample any wines you think you might like, and buy according to your own storage capacity.

DOC (*Denominazione di Origine Controllata*)

See Italian labelling regulations.

Dôle

The red table wine of Switzerland made in the Valais. It is a fairly dry, warm, scented Burgundy type. Good ordinary wine for everyday drinking.

Domaine

A word used to describe certain wine estates in France.

Dom Pérignon

A seventeenth-century monk who lived and experimented at Hautvillers in the midst of the French Champagne vineyards. He is credited with inventing the method of stopping bottles with a tight cork so as to contain the seven atmospheres of pressure naturally created by carbon dioxide during the secondary fermentation of his local wine. This procedure guaranteed that the bubbles would stay in what is now called Champagne. Luckily for Moët et Chandon, the Dom's former abbey now belongs to them, and his name today graces the bottles of their finest brand.

Eastern Europe

Czechoslovakia, Hungary, Romania, Bulgaria and East Germany all produce wine in quantities often only sufficient for local consumption. Some of them are exporting wines (Hungary and Bulgaria especially) that are rather heavy and often too sweet for Western tastes. A large part of their export is to Russia and other Eastern (Warsaw Pact) countries.

Bulgaria is actually the world's fourth largest exporter of wine. Its Mavrud and Cabernet Sauvignon need to be opened well before drinking, as is true of all such inexpensive, robust red wines. Hungary makes good white and red table wines. Yugoslavia, if considered East European, is the area's largest producer. (See separate entries.)

Edelfäule

German for noble rot. Edel means noble, *fäule,* rot. (See also Noble rot.)

Edelzwicker

Noble 'mixture' is the name of one of the most basic white wines of Alsace, made from a mixture of noble grapes, including mainly Sylvaner and Pinot Blanc. It is table wine with a clean Alsace 'nose', but less characteristic than those made from single grape varieties. It is light and usually good.

EEC (European Economic Community)

The EEC has done much to codify and standardize the methods its members must employ for qualifying their wines. It divides wine into two categories, Table and Quality, and sets standards for judging them. Maximum yields are set for quality wine production, bottle sizes are regulated and there are rules for labelling.

The European wine laws are still being developed, and though they cause some headaches for producers, will surely, in the long run, bring benefits to the consumer by rationalizing the ways in which wines are to be described. EEC wine rules also cover general production methods, yields and measurements throughout the community. Each country adds specific laws to cover its own wine needs.

Egypt

As is proven by the hieroglyphic pictographs in Egypt, wine was known there well before classical days and before its production became perfected in Europe. From the beginning of this century, a small amount of wine has been produced from vineyards near Alexandria. Cru des Ptolemées and Reine Cléopâtre are the best-known white wines; Omar Khayyam the best red.

Eiswein

A uniquely German quality designation for a special category of QmP wine. It applies to wine made from grapes that have been left on the vine until as late as December or January. Occasionally a cold snap will freeze the grapes on the vines. It is possible, then, to pick them early in the morning while still frozen and crush them immediately. Because sugar helps prevent freezing, the least ripe grapes will be icier than the riper ones. Thus, when crushed, the first run of juice will be only from the ripest grapes with the most concentrated sweetness – almost a sugar syrup. This is the juice that is then fermented into Eiswein, while the rest of the less ripe grapes and their ice are discarded. The result is a lusciously sweet, smooth, dessert wine with a high acidity – an expensive curiosity.

Emilia-Romagna

An area south of the River Po in Italy, from which comes red Lambrusco, Albana di Romagna, a semi-sweet white wine,

and Trebbiano di Romagna, straw-coloured, dry and
agreeable.

England

Although wine has been made in England since at least the
days of the Venerable Bede, about AD 720, and Alfred the
Great passed protective laws for its growers, the EEC today
regards the UK as an experimental area. It grants UK
producers special terms to help them develop their wines.

The largest vineyard in England still only covers some 14
hectares (35 acres), and total national production is about
7,000 hectolitres (154,000 gallons). English wines are mainly
white, light and dry, the best rather like those of Alsace in
character. Because of England's uncertain climate, its wines
tend to be acid and usually need chaptalization to raise the
alcoholic content of their must (see Chaptalization). Vines
are grown in the southern and eastern counties for the most
part. (English wine is not to be confused with 'British wine',
which is sweet stuff made from fermented, imported juice
concentrate, alas!)

Épernay

An important centre for the French Champagne industry;
headquarters for the producers' association, the *Comité
Interprofessionnel du Vin de Champagne* (CIVC).

Erzeugerabfüllung

The German equivalent of *mise en bouteille à la domaine*,
meaning bottled by the producer.

Fendant

The delightful, ubiquitous, light white wine of the Valais in
Switzerland. Probably the best manifestation of a good wine
made from the otherwise undistinguished Chasselas grape.
It is very pleasant with Swiss lake fish, and is drunk almost
as universally as water in Switzerland.

Fermentation

Wine cannot be made without fermentation, a natural
process that man can only aid, control or speed up. Grape
juice acquires natural yeast during pressing, because grape
skins have a powdery yeast dust on them. The yeast
converts the grape juice's natural sugar into alcohol, giving
off carbon dioxide, making a drier, and different, liquid. This
happens with fruit of any kind. Man's role in this is to
control the fermentation so that what results is an
agreeable drinking liquid.

  Modern wine-makers leave as little as possible to chance.
Fermentation is allowed to continue until all sugar is used
up, leaving a dry wine, or the fermentation is stopped,
leaving the wine sweet.

  Malolactic fermentation (if you like sounding like a wine
expert) indicates an acid fermentation that usually happens
in the spring after a vintage. Wine contains malic acid, the
sourness of unripe fruit. The fermentation is useful because
it changes the malic to milder lactic acid. If this happens
after the wine is bottled, the gas produced cannot escape
and the wine becomes very slightly sparkling.

Fining

It may sound crazy, but fining used to mean the addition of
egg white or ox blood to new wine so that sediment in the
wine would attach itself to the egg white (most of which was
imported from China, by the way) and thus fall to the
bottom of the container. Once this had happened, the wine
could be drawn off, purified of sediment.

  Today this age-old process is generally accomplished by
using a substance most of us have never heard of and
couldn't describe – bentonite. All wines need to be 'fined'
within a few months of fermentation and filtered to keep

them stable. To make doubly sure that there are no foreign substances in the wine, it is filtered again before it is bottled. What you get, in both cases, is the purest possible wine, but this does not mean that the wine so treated is necessarily a 'fine' wine!

Fino

The driest version of Spanish Sherry. You can call for 'uno fino' in any Spanish *tapa* bar and not only be given a cold glass of this dry, pale, delicate wine, but a selection of little bite-sized snacks, called *tapas*, to chew on while doing so. Fino is the wino's answer to Dry Martini – *the* apéritif. Best-known brands are La Ina and Tio Pepe.

Fleurie

The lovely name of one of the nine famous villages of Beaujolais in the north of the region. The wine is one of the lightest of *grand cru* Beaujolais wines; fruity and fresh. The grape is the Gamay.

Flor

A curious fungus, or wine-yeast, that lies thickly on top of wine and causes it to oxidize more slowly than usual. This was for many years the exclusive and unpredictable secret of the Spanish Sherry industry. It was a natural phenomenon, and uncontrollable. Recently it has been more or less harnessed as a result of scientific

investigations, and is now being used in Cyprus, South Africa and in California to produce 'sherries' that are beginning to have some resemblance to the wines they are trying to imitate.

If you want the real taste of Sherry, I advise sticking to the Spanish version, expensive though it is.

Food and wine to go with it

Companionate food and drink is always a delectable subject. What should one drink with what food?

Actually there are no strict rules, only the experience of centuries to guide you. Generally speaking, white wines seem to taste better with fish and white meats; red wines with red meat and game. Light white wines are excellent with shellfish. But there's no reason not to have red wine with chicken or turkey or pork, if you want to. Some of the more flavourful fish are even fine with light red wine – salmon or red mullet, say. Use rosé when you can't make up your mind!

Sparkling wines seem to go well with almost any kind of food. You can drink Champagne throughout a meal with no ill-effect. Champagne is an exception, too, to the 'rule' that your wines should improve as a meal goes along. The king of wines makes a good apéritif before meals, as well as an excellent ending.

In France, where both food and wine are important subjects, many wine buffs pick their wines first, and then decide what to eat with it. There are some belly-filling French restaurants – good, but more gourmand than gourmet – where they place a bottle of ordinary red, white and rosé on the table, and you simply help yourself to what you prefer.

Cheese goes particularly well with wines. A blue cheese (Roquefort, especially) can take a fine sweet wine like a Sauternes, or a hearty, fortified wine like Port. Milder cheeses (Pont l'Évêque, Camembert) call for Burgundy or Bordeaux. Good, smelly American Liederkranz or German Limburger are beautiful with a powerful red Cabernet Sauvignon from California.

If you are holding a real party and time and hangovers are no problem, the sweet wines of Sauternes can be a capital way to end a meal. Château d'Yquem is the world's best sweet white wine, but it is also one of its most expensive. A good Château La Tour Blanche, a bit less costly, or Hungarian Tokay, or a German *Trockenbeerenauslese* are all very acceptable substitutes. The British like fortified wines such as Port and Madeira with dessert or after the meal. All of these can be delicious drunk for their own sakes, without food.

Fortified wines

Sherry, Port, Madeira. Fortified wines are any that have been strengthened with a dose of extra alcohol, usually a spirit made from distilled wine. Their alcoholic content is high; between 15 per cent for light Sherries to 20 per cent or more for Port. Imitations of true Sherry and Port abound, but none can really stand up to the quality and flavour of the original.

There are other fortified wines: Vermouth was originally made with wormwood, the derivation of its name, which used to be a main ingredient of these wines. Vermouths are all flavoured, fortified wines. The Italian type is mostly red and sweet. The French type is white and dry, even bitter. French Noilly-Prat and Chambéry are the most delicate and subtle of them.

In addition, there is Marsala from Sicily, used mainly in cooking today; Málaga from Spain; various southern French wines or *vins doux naturels*, such as Muscat-de-Beaumes-de-Venise; and Banyuls from near the Spanish border.

Frais

French for cool. What light red wines and all white ones should be when brought to the table. (See Temperatures.)

France

France has nearly 1.2 million hectares (3 million acres) of vines under cultivation (0.8 million hectares less than 100 years ago, but producing one-third more wine). The best of French wines, especially their reds and Champagnes, are superior to those of any other place of origin, and very few white wines in the world are better than French whites, except perhaps some in the sweeter categories.

The average Frenchman, however, never tastes a great wine, for of the 75 million hectolitres (1½ billion gallons) of wine they make yearly, four-fifths is just nameless, drinkable, ordinary table wine. The other fifth is the best – *Appellation Contrôlée* (AC), or *Vins Délimités de Qualité Supérieure* (VDQS) – controlled by government regulations.

Long before the nineteenth century when Bordeaux wines were classified (or ossified, as some people believe) into nearly immutable rankings, wine was being made in France. The first French wine region was probably the Greek colony of Marseille, and up the Rhône from there. The Romans imported Gallic wine, called *picatum*, for which shipments the Gauls invented the first wooden wine casks to replace Roman *amphorae*. Eventually they discovered that wood changed and improved the flavour of wine. Later the famous French scientist Louis Pasteur discovered how to keep wine from going bad by pasteurizing it, and a French chemist, Dr Chaptal, found he could save wine that had insufficient natural alcohol by adding sugar to the must.

These improvements finally brought mass production and the reduction of most wine to an average common denominator of quality. *Vin ordinaire* is easier to make than Château Margaux, with its labour-intensive ruthless pruning and selective picking. Standardization means you can now drive into a Provençal winery and ask them to fill up your 25-litre (5½-gallon) *bidon* with good, cheap wine as easily as you can buy petrol. Nevertheless, wine-making in France still remains a craft. Over one-sixth of the French population works in wine in one way or another, and each Frenchman consumes some 115 litres (25 gallons) of it yearly.

Among the best wine-producing regions in France are: Bordeaux, Burgundy, the Rhône, the Loire, Alsace, Champagne, South-west France, Languedoc-Roussillon (The Midi) and Provence (see individual entries).

Frascati

The white wine from the hills south of Rome, where the Pope has his summer residence. It is light, soft, pale-green, grapy and very agreeable with summer foods, especially on the shores of the Mediterranean. My favourite is Fontana Candida.

French labelling regulations

The French, quite appropriately, started regulating wine labels in the 1930s (in Châteauneuf-du-Pape) and theirs is still one of the simplest systems. Classification as shown on French labels begins with *vin de table*, or wine for ordinary consumption. Next up the scale, and better than the table wine, is *vin de pays* (table wine plus a geographical location name). Next comes VDQS (*Vin Délimité de Qualité Supérieure*), which indicates better quality wine. At the top are AOC or simply AC (*Appellation d'Origine Contrôlée*, or *Appellation Contrôlée*), meaning wines whose origins are supervised.

Geographical places of origin of all AC wines must be declared. Each vineyard is allowed only a maximum yield. The alcoholic strength of the wine must be of a certain level, and the way the wine is made is also specified. The appellation can cover a whole region, like AC Beaujolais, for example, or a very specific area within that part. (Appellation Margaux Contrôlée is certain to be better wine than one that merely claims an AC Bordeaux.) So, for the best French wines (except for Champagne) look for AOC or AC on the labels, followed by one or more specified regional names.

52

Generic wine

A term used to separate traditional, geographical names for wine types from those produced in newer wine areas. The objective is to prevent the confusion that was caused when newer wine-growing regions, like the USA and Australia, started to call their wines 'Burgundy', or 'Chablis', when they had little or no resemblance to the originals, even though they might in themselves be very good wines. The practice began as a way to give prospective purchasers at least a vague idea of what style of wine they were buying.

Most countries, apart from the USA, now accept that wines like Port, Sherry or Champagne are unique, and their names legitimately belong to the places where such wines originated. The same is true for other specific French, German or Italian wines such as Sauternes, Côtes du Rhône, Chablis, Rhine Wine and Chianti. American and Australian wine-growers at first resisted this tendency, but many other non-European vintners now appear to realize that their wines are good enough to stand by their own appellations, or by varietal names. The tendency to borrow names from European wines is gradually fading away, to the benefit of both old and new.

German labelling regulations

German wine quality is based initially on the natural sugar content in the grape juice and starts with *Tafelwein*. This indicates a light, agreeable, ordinary wine, but one that must be made from an approved grape variety and from one of the table wine areas, i.e. the Mosel, Rhein, Main, Neckar or Oberrhein. The next grade up is *Landwein*, and equivalent to French *vin de pays*. These are new dry wines that must be *trocken* or *halbtrocken*. They account for 15 per cent of total German wine production – a result of growing demand for drier wine.

Next comes *Qualitätswein bestimmter Anbaugebiete* (QbA). According to German regulations, these are quality wines with a higher sugar content in the must and with typical regional flavour. A *Qualitätswein* must come from one of the 11 quality wine regions (Ahr, Mosel-Saar-Ruwer, Mittelrhein, Rheingau, Nahe, Rheinhessen, Rheinpfalz, Hessische Bergstrasse, Württemberg, Baden and Franken), from

recognized grape varieties. Minimum alcohol content is
around nine per cent. All *Qualitätswein* undergoes rigid
government tests, the result of which is shown in a long
number beginning with the letters AP that must appear on
the label.

Qualitätswein mit Prädikat (QmP) is the highest quality wine
category and gets special grading. This quality is divided
into six grades. The lightest is *Kabinett*; next comes *Spätlese* or
late harvest, so slightly sweet; then *Auslese* or selective
harvest; *Beerenauslese*, from individually selected grape
berries; and a dessert wine, *Trockenbeerenauslese*, made from
grapes left on the vine until they are like raisins, is rare,
delicious and very expensive; and finally *Eiswein* from grapes
that are frozen, even rarer and equally costly. All QmP wines
must also show AP numbers.

Germany

Germans seem to be less interested in drinking their own
wines than are the citizens of many another country. They
produce far less wine than Portugal, and they themselves
drink less wine per capita (about 22 litres/39 pints) than
even their conservative neighbours the Swiss.

Only about 15 per cent of German wine is red, the rest all
white, with Riesling grapes the 'noblest' and most used for
wine making. German wines are delicate, refreshing and low
in alcohol.

German vines cling for protection from the cold to those
areas close to water, such as the Rhine, the Mosel and their
tributaries, the Main, the Neckar, the Nahe, the Ahr and
along the banks of Lake Constance. This liquid scenery
provides some of the most beautiful tourist areas of Europe,
littered with romantic, ruined castles, quaint villages and
sites like those where river sprites revelled and where the
Rhine Maidens used to lure sailors to a seductive doom.

German vineyards range from the low, rolling hills of the
south to steep, cliff-like banks along the Rhine and the
Mosel farther north. In some places the slopes have a
gradient of 70 degrees. The vines nearer the water do best;
those over 600 metres (1,968 feet) high up on the cliffsides
tend to be less productive. The rivers help to keep
temperatures temperate and the mists that float off them
also retain warmth for the comfort of the vine.

Germany's wine-producing area is not only located north of most others but is comparatively small. Nevertheless, the wines it produces are some of the finest anywhere – light and fragrant. Rhine wines are inclined to be slightly heavier and more fruity than Mosels. Most German wines are meant to be drunk soon after bottling – the kind of wine you can buy on your way home from the office and enjoy that evening. The green-bottled ones are from the Mosel-Saar-Ruwer; the brown bottles from the Rhine. A small quantity, from Franken (or Franconia), is put up in flagon-shaped green bottles. It is a dry, more robust, earthier wine.

Gevrey-Chambertin

One of the most famous villages of the Côte d'Or in Burgundy. It used to be called simply Gevrey, but added Chambertin to its name because that is the most famous vineyard of the area. Wines sold as Gevrey-Chambertin are good secondary, regional wines. Better are Gevrey-Chambertin *premiers crus* (with the name of the vineyard after) and better still are the *grands crus*, which are very noble wines indeed. Of them, Chambertin-Clos de Bèze is tops, and very costly.

Gewürztraminer

As wine, this refers to a highly fruity, aromatic rather 'soft' wine, with a pale-pinkish tinge. It is made from the grape of the same name. *Gewürz* means 'spicy' in German. It is not a subtle wine, but often makes a beautiful accompaniment for spicy dishes, cheese or meat. The German ones are inclined to be cloyingly sweet. I prefer the drier Alsatian version.

Glasses

There is no doubt that wine tastes better, or at least appears to, in elegant, thin glasses. The ideal glass is a stemmed one for all kinds of wine (and for most other drinks as well). The stem allows you to hold the glass without heating its contents with your hand. Some people even drink chilled white wines or Champagnes while holding the glass by its base, thus maintaining total insulation. Avoid the flat Champagne glass because it loses the wine's sparkle fast, and it is very easy to spill and waste fine wine from it.

Eye appeal is important. The French *Institut National des Appellations d'Origine*, which should know, recommends one basic design that can be used for any wine. It is stemmed, with a slightly tulip-shaped, elongated bowl, the glass sloping in towards the rim so as to concentrate the wine's bouquet. It is both good-looking and elegant.

Glasses should be clear, not coloured. Even so-called 'white' wines have subtle variations of pale yellow and green that are lost inside a pink or green glass. German wine glasses sometimes vary their colouring by having the stems, rather than the bowls, coloured. This at least leaves the wine to show its own hues. Glasses should also be unadorned with cutting or engraving.

But if someone offers you a drink in a thimble-sized liqueur-glass, or a blue one or a deeply cut antique, don't hesitate to accept it. It takes more than a mere glass to spoil a good wine.

Grand cru

The French words for a best growth vineyard and that vineyard's wine. It is used mostly by the top vineyards of Burgundy.

Grape varieties

Several elements go into the making of wine: good grapes, know-how and the skills and integrity of the wine-maker. But the greatest of these, and the most important, is the grape itself, for in the grape lies 100 per cent of the potential quality of the wine. In the making of wine, it is hardly possible to add anything to a grape's quality. The best

cellarman is one who manages to lose the least part of that elusive character.

Wine has been around since at least 3000 BC and there are over 3,000 grape varieties. Some grapes have a dozen different names, depending on the areas in which they are grown. A few of the most important of them, however, I give below:

Aligoté A Burgundy grape making good, dry white wine (see also Aligoté). Also grown in Russia.

Barbera Red wine grape from Piedmont in Italy, also used in California. The dark, full-bodied wine (good with pasta) made from it is also called Barbera.

Cabernet A grape variety with two important strains. Cabernet Franc is used for Loire red wines (and to some extent in Bordeaux). Cabernet Sauvignon (often called simply 'Cabernet') is the great grape of Bordeaux Médoc red wines, and is also used for some of the best Californian, Australian, South American and other wines. It produces tough but top-quality wines that usually need ageing to reach their best drinking level.

Chardonnay The main grape used for white Burgundy and in Champagne. Makes dry, rich, complex wine. Also used in other parts of France, Italy, California, Eastern Europe, South Africa, South America and Australia.

Chasselas A white wine grape, best known for producing the ubiquitous light white of Switzerland, Fendant.

Chenin Blanc Number one grape for white Loires like Vouvray

and Saumur, and some Californian wines. It can produce fine sweet wines (Quarts de Chaume) as well as dry ones. It is also grown in South Africa.

Folle Blanche White grape producing the wine distilled into Cognac in France; better in California. Acid.

Gamay Excellent red wine grape, used almost exclusively for Beaujolais. It is also used in California for superior wines and called Gamay-Beaujolais – not to be confused with wine called simply 'Gamay'. (An example of the unpredictability of some US nomenclature.)

Gewürztraminer A pinkish grape used mainly in Alsace, Germany and California. It produces a very perfumed white wine; some think it's a bit overpowering, both as to taste and aroma. The best wine from this grape is made in Alsace, though the German equivalent is also excellent. Used in Eastern Europe, California and Australia.

Grenache Good-quality grape used (among others) for reds in southern France, for Châteauneuf-du-Pape, for example, in Spain for Rioja and in California.

Grüner Veltliner Mainly in Austria for light, white wines for drinking young.

Malvasia White grape used today mainly for making Madeira. The Greeks used it in Homeric times and took it with them to their Mediterranean colonies.

Merlot Good grape used in Bordeaux for reds, particularly in Saint Émilion and Pomerol. Lends softness and charm to blends with other famous grapes. Also grown in Italy, Switzerland and Chile. Fruity bouquet.

Müller-Thurgau Cross between Riesling and Sylvaner. Leading type for German Rhine wines and in Austria and the UK. Makes soft, fruity white wines.

Muscadet Grape from Burgundy, originally named 'Melon'. Used almost exclusively for Muscadet wine, a light dry white wine produced near Nantes in the Loire. Popular in Europe since World War II.

Muscat (Moscato) A sweet grape used mainly for dessert wines (Muscat-de-Beaumes-de-Venise is one well-known product). In Alsace it produces a dry, fruity wine. A very small quantity of excellent *eau-de-vie* is also made from it in France.

Nebbiolo Italy's top red wine grape, grown in Piedmont and responsible for Barolo, Barbaresco and Gattinara. Its name derives from the Italian for fog (*nebbia*) because it ripens well in the mists around Barolo in September.

Pedro Ximénez A variety brought to Spain from Germany by a man named Peter Siemens, whose name was Hispanicized. It is used there for sweetening Sherry and Montilla. Also used in California, Australia and South Africa. (Often written as 'PX'.)

Pinot A very popular and productive family of wine grape used all over the world under various pseudonyms.

Pinot Noir is a top-quality grape used in Burgundy for fine red wines. It is also the main grape used for Champagne. It is grown in California, Austria, Hungary and Switzerland. In Germany it is called Spätburgunder, and in Switzerland Rotklevner.

Pinot Gris is called Ruländer in Germany, Pinot Grigio in Italy and Tokay in Alsace. It is a cousin of the Blanc and Noir versions. The best Pinot Gris wine is German from around Baden.

Pinot Blanc is grown in Alsace, and Italy, where it is called Pinot Bianco. (The Pinot-Chardonnay of California is really Chardonnay, not a Pinot, though it may be a distant cousin.)

Riesling Famous in Alsace and Germany, especially in Mosel, Rheingau and Rheinhessen. Used in almost all wine-growing countries. A great white wine grape, known since Roman days. Makes good wines also in Austria, California, Chile, Italy and Switzerland. Light white wines, with a good balance between sweet and dry in Germany, mostly dry elsewhere.

Sauvignon Blanc Excellent in dry white Pouilly-Fumé. It is also known as Blanc-Fumé and, perversely, in the USA as

Fumé-Blanc. It is used in Bordeaux for dry white wines, as well as in semi-sweet Graves, in sweet Sauternes and lovely dry Loire wines. It has a distinct smoky-fruity aroma. It also appears in Italy, Eastern Europe and in California, where its product is heavier, but still distinctively 'herby'.

Sémillon Subject to noble rot, this white wine grape contributes to the unctious sweetness of Sauternes.

Steen A South African grape which is probably a relative of the Loire valley grape, Chenin Blanc. In South Africa it makes crisp, dry wines, something like those of the Loire.

Sylvaner A grape used widely in Germany, Austria, California and Alsace for white wines. It is at its best in Alsace, where it is turned into a very fine, fresh, fruity wine. Elsewhere it produces light, soft, short-lived but pleasant wines; not as distinguished as Riesling.

Syrah Best grape for Rhône red wines (Hermitage, etc.). High in tannin. Used in Australia as Shiraz (the Iranian city whence it is supposed to have originated).

Traminer This variety is no longer recognized, being officially listed these days as Gewürztraminer.

Trebbiano One of the grapes with a dozen names! Used in Italy for Orvieto, Soave, wine for making brandy and in many other white wines. It becomes Ugni Blanc in southern France, Saint Émilion in Cognac. Very acid, white wines.

Verdicchio A good Italian white wine grape and the good wine made from it.

Vernaccia This grape is very high in natural alcohol (17 per cent and over) and comes from Sardinia and Tuscany. The wine is dry and aromatic.

Zinfandel A Californian exclusivity! Makes heavy, dark, fruity wine with a good bouquet. An import from Europe in the middle of the last century, but from where is a mystery.

Greece

The Greeks, even in Homeric days, drank wine, and the country still produces double the amount made in Germany. Her most famous product is *retsina* with its distinctive pine resin taste. When not too highly resinated, and nicely chilled, this can be a refreshing drink in hot weather. Otherwise, Greek wines are rather high in alcohol, and are inclined to be rough and to lack finesse.

Grillet, Château

The smallest appellation in France with just 2.4 hectares (6 acres), producing a distinctive white wine from the unusual Viognier grape in the northern Rhône.

Groot Constantia

Probably the only really handsome headquarters of a national Oenological and Viticultural Research Institute in existence. Groot Constantia is a proud South African wine estate near Capetown at Stellenbosch. The house is an extraordinarily beautiful Dutch-Colonial style, one-time home, that began as a simple farm in 1685. In 1734, Carl-Georg Wieser switched the farm's purpose to growing grape vines. A later owner, a member of a prominent South African family, Hendrik Cloote, made such good wines there that the name Constantia became famous almost worldwide.

The estate, which is in lovely countryside, has been government property since 1875 and produces excellent reds and some good whites. It is now a national monument.

Hangover cures

Alcohol and wines undoubtedly do cause headaches in imbibers, due usually to overindulgence or smoke-filled rooms. Fill up with Vitamin C or a couple of aspirins before retiring. Some drinkers allege that the unfortunate state of hangover can be alleviated to some extent by various bartenders' soothing recipes. Most of these contain Fernet Branca and peppermint. Drink as much water as you can before going to bed, which won't keep you up, because your condition presupposes considerable dehydration.

Preventive measures include drinking milk or a spoonful of olive oil before a party, or a non-alcoholic cocktail like Pussyfoot: 1 ounce each lemon, orange, lime juice, 1 dash grenadine, 1 egg yolk, shaken with ice, strained into a glass and topped with soda water. The famous 'hair-of-the-dog' is not recommended by those who know! However, if you stick *exclusively* to Champagne I find you suffer no after-effects. But that may be purely personal.

Harvest

A happy time in a vineyard when the grapes are being gathered, beginning in September in some areas, and lasting in others sometimes (to obtain Germany's *Eiswein*) into January. Being a seasonal job, workers are often imported from other countries. France imports labour from Spain and Portugal and California brings in workers from Mexico, for example. *Vendangeurs* are often youngsters who live communally in barracks. They work hard during three or four weeks, but their life can be full of singing and dancing and old-time farm-life fun as well (see also Vintage).

Haut-Brion, Château

This powerful, distinguished Bordeaux first growth (a Graves, and now American-owned) was Talleyrand's secret weapon. He used the wine to help penetrate the defences of rival diplomats, so as to coax secrets from them. He found this manoeuvre so successful that he bought the property. Even today, it is unquestionably a great wine (see Bordeaux). La Mission Haut-Brion, once a rival, is now under the same ownership.

Health

Modern medicine is beginning to agree that alcohol taken as wine (where it is in about a ten to 12 per cent solution) is an ideal treatment for several ills of man. The French doctor E. A. Maury, in *Wine is the Best Medicine*, says that 'two grammes of alcohol per kilo of bodyweight can constitute a beneficial reserve nutriment without producing metabolic modifications'. (That is, no hangover or unpleasant after-effects.) Then he goes on to give specific recommendations of wines for maladies, such as Alsace for high blood pressure, Anjou for loss of appetite, Bordeaux for depression and a score of other things, Médoc for tonsillitis (!), Burgundy for old age, Champagne for rheumatism, and Loire for reducing cholesterol, to give a few examples.

Dr. Salvatore Lucia of the University of California Medical School, in *Wine and Wellbeing*, finds wine better than pills for relaxation therapy, and recommends one to four ounces a meal. Dr. C. D. Leake agrees with Maury that wine is good for high blood pressure and heart disease. Other doctors say wine's content of vitamins, enzymes, minerals and aldehydes make it an excellent drink for people who have trouble absorbing fats (which includes most people over forty). Doctors at the Cardiff Medical Research Council believe their investigations show that wine-drinking people have fewer heart attacks.

Hectare

An area of 10,000 square metres (about 2.5 acres). European vineyards are usually measured in hectares.

Hectolitre

One hundred litres metric, 22 gallons (UK) and about 26 gallons (USA). Usually shortened to 'hecto' in vintner's parlance.

Hermitage

A great wine from the Rhône valley some 80 kilometres (50 miles) south of Lyon. About two-thirds is red and one-third white. The white is pale-golden, dry, with a great bouquet.

The red Hermitage is one of the world's top wines. Made from Syrah grapes, it is deep red and ages well. Tain, the village it comes from, is now known as Tain-l'Hermitage in honour of its wine.

The banks of the Rhône are steeply terraced here and south-facing. They have grown vines since before the Romans invaded. Rain over the centuries has washed the thin topsoil down to the bottom of the slopes, so today it must be carried back up and respread after heavy storms. But it still produces wonderful wines.

Crozes-Hermitage is a wider vineyard area around Hermitage. The wines are similar, and sometimes excellent, but less concentrated.

The unknown hermit of Hermitage is supposed to have been hiding from Roman invaders on top of the hill where it is now grown. He became very thirsty and, miraculously, God sent him a group of wine-growers (since, naturally, all good wine-growers went to heaven). They planted grape vines which grew and ripened overnight. The hermit, praising God with each sip, continued to drink Hermitage for the rest of his life.

Heurige

Fresh, sprightly young wine. *Heurigen* are the open-air wine gardens just outside Vienna in which they are served. Beethoven, Mozart, Schubert and Strauss were inspired by both, the Viennese claim, or by the atmosphere they helped to create.

Hock

An English term for Rhine wines, supposedly because their first impact on the United Kingdom's people was through wines imported from Hochheim, one of the Rhine villages.

Hungary

Hungary is rich in indigenous vines not found elsewhere in the world, Kadarka for red wine, Furmint for Tokay and Harslevelü for whites, among others.

Best-known wines outside Hungary are Olasz Riesling and Bull's Blood.

Israel

The Bible makes it clear that wine has been made in what is now Israel for centuries. The country has a small production of some 450,000 hectolitres (9,900,000 gallons) of mostly rather sweetish wines, though the trend is towards drier types recently.

Italian labelling regulations

Italy passed a tough wine law in 1963. Italian wine names are either geographical or they indicate the main grape used. If the same grape is used widely, the place name is added (Barbera d'Alba, for example).

Basic Italian wine is called *vino da tavola*, though the Italians have recently approved a new category, *vino tipico*, similar to French *vin de pays* and German *Landwein*.

There are two categories of quality wine, *Denominazione di Origine Controllata* (DOC) and *Denominazione di Origine Controllata e Garantita* (DOCG). Only four wines so far have made the top category: Barolo, Barbaresco, Vino Nobile di Montepulciano and Brunello di Montalcino. (Chianti Classico is expected to join the list in 1985.) All aspects of cultivation, production and sales are tightly controlled.

Vintage is indicated by the word 'Vendemmia' and the date. The words 'Vecchio' (old) or 'Riserva' (reserve) refer to the length of ageing in barrel and in bottle. 'Classico' means the wine comes from the heart of a traditional production area (Chianti Classico). Wine-makers are not allowed to use words like 'Extra', 'Fine', 'Selezionato'. A DOC wine can be counted on to be what it says it is.

Italy

The largest producer and exporter of wine in the world, Italy is covered with vineyards and makes about one-fifth of the total world production of wine. Italians are prodigious consumers of their own product, too – 110 litres (24 gallons) per head yearly of extremely drinkable wine. Some of it is of high quality, although the majority, since it is made to be consumed with food, is ordinary table wine.

Some of the best-known and better Italian red wines are Barolo, Valpolicella, Lambrusco and Chianti. Of the whites

Soave, Verdicchio, Orvieto and Frascati are among the most popular.

The Italians make their wines to be enjoyed with food. Most of them are regional in character and their variety is partly due to specific mixtures of grapes (not blends of wines) in proportions that have been handed down from father to son over centuries. Most Italian wines are meant to be drunk within three years.

Jerez

The Spanish word for Sherry, made in the southern Spanish town of the same name. Jerez vineyards are spread in a triangle between the small port of Sanlúcar de Barrameda, and another small port, Puerto de Santa Maria. Sanlúcar was the port from which Columbus set sail on his third voyage to the New World. One of his original ships was named *Santa Maria*. Jerez is also famed for raising fighting bulls and beautiful horses. The 'Spanish Horses' of Vienna were originally from this part of Spain, known as *Jerezanos*.

Francis Drake gave England's love affair with Sherry a big boost. He raided Cádiz in 1587 and sailed off with 2,900 pipes of it (each holding about 500 litres/110 gallons) to England. As a Spanish authority commented, 'That demonstrated, once again, the good taste the British have always shown.'

Johannisberg

A small Rheingau village in Germany with a famous castle, Schloss Johannisberg, at the top of the hill behind the Johannisberg vineyard. The Riesling wines from the Schloss

are among the best in Germany. The castle boasts only 35 hectares (87 acres) so its product is rarely to be found, since it is all snapped up by its German fans and a few privileged gourmet restaurants. The castle itself is inhabited and presents a very impressive silhouette against the Rhine sky.

Johannisberg is also used as a general name on labels of Rheingau wines, which can be described as Bereich Johannisberg. Without the word 'schloss' the wine may come from any Rheingau village, but will not be of the quality of 'schloss' wine.

The Swiss confusingly make a 'Johannisberger' wine from Sylvaner grapes. Californians add to the confusion by calling the German Riesling grape 'Johannisberger Riesling'

Jug wines

Much of today's table wine now comes in jugs of 150 to 300 centilitres (2.6 to 5.2 pints). These are intended to be drunk almost immediately, so they are not stoppered with cork but usually have screw or cap tops. In the USA, outsized jug wines are extremely popular, and they seem to be becoming more so in the UK as well. The French often buy very large containers of *vin ordinaire*, 25 litres (5½ gallons) or more, in plastic jerry can-type containers, which they bottle themselves at home. For quick-drinking Italian wines, these bigger bottles and containers also seem to be the trend in recent years.

Juliénas

Half a million gallons of this excellent *grand cru* Beaujolais flows out to an appreciative drinking world yearly. Vigorous and fruity, it is one of the best wines of the area.

Jura

A small French wine area near the Swiss border. Its best-known product is Rosé d'Arbois, among the best of pinks and sometimes called 'Pelure d'Oignon' (onion-skin) because of its colour. Arbois also applies to Jura red and white wines, which King Henry IV of France considered 'lip-smackin' good'. An unusual golden, sweet Jura wine, Château-Chalon, can be delicious too.

Kabinett

After *Tafelwein*, *Qualitätswein bestimmter Anbaugebiete* (QbA) comes *Qualitätswein mit Prädikat* (QmP), which is the top grade in the German hierarchy of wines. There are six levels of the highest quality and *Kabinett* is the first rung of that ladder. It is usually medium-dry, light, elegant and a good buy (see also German labelling regulations).

Krug

A small but very fine French Champagne house. Joseph Krug, a German, founded the firm in about 1845 in Reims.

Also, Charles Krug of California, who planted an early vineyard, and began making sparkling wine in the Napa Valley in 1858, only 13 years after his Frenchified namesake had founded the Champagne house in France. Now one of the best of American sparklers.

KWV (*Ko-operatieve Wijnbouwers Vereniging*)

The national wine co-operative of South Africa at Paarl. It controls minimum prices for wines, sets production quotas, tells wine merchants how much they must pay for wines in low production years, and handles financial transactions between producers and buyers.

71

Labelling

Labelling regulations in most countries change faster than a chameleon changes colour. Rules have become much stricter in the years since World War II. The EEC is trying to match up the regulations of various countries. Meantime, the wine-producing nations have a Babel of label rules. (See the entries on French, German, Italian and Spanish labelling regulations for an explanation of the more important rules.)

Lacrima Christi

A poetic Latin name (meaning 'tears of Christ') for an unfortunately rather pedestrian Italian wine made on the slopes of Mount Vesuvius.

Lafite-Rothschild, Château

One of the four first growths of the 1855 classification of Médoc wines in the commune of Pauillac. Owned by Baron Elie de Rothschild. It is Claret at its finest.

Lambrusco

A 'pizza wine', very popular in the USA, made in northern Italy along the Po River. It is, however, looked down upon in its native Italy. It gives a deep, purplish wine that froths when poured, the bubbles quickly subsiding to leave a slight prickling sensation on the tongue. Not a great wine, but one to be drunk young, with food. (It is made into an absolutely marvellous vinegar called Balsamico di Modena.) The DOC versions are usually dry, and must have at least 10.5 degrees of alcohol. Vines are grown high on trellises. Lambrusco is also the name of a grape variety.

Landwein

See German labelling regulations.

Languedoc-Roussillon

The area largely responsible for France's 'wine lake', the appropriately liquid way some people refer to the oceans of

ordinary wine that flow from this, one of the world's most productive of wine areas. It consists of four French *départements* – the Gard, Hérault, Aude and Pyrenées Orientales. This chunk of *la belle France* alone holds about five per cent of the wine-growing territory of the whole world! It is full of co-operatives, largely because a majority of its wine-growers own less than five hectares (twelve acres) of land, and only a quarter of them own more than 50 hectares (123 acres). These establishments sometimes achieve up to 200 hectolitres (4,400 gallons) of wine per hectare, an astonishing yield.

The largest part of all this wine is very mediocre, red *vin ordinaire*. But a good deal of effort is going into improving the quality of its *vins de pays* and *vins de table*. Among the best wines of the area are:

Côteaux du Languedoc; *Corbières* and *Corbières Supérieur*; *Minervois*; *Fitou*; *Blanquette de Limoux* (sparkling); *Roussillon*; and *Banyuls*, *Rivesaultes* and *Maury* (which are *vins doux naturels*).

Latour, Château

One of the four first growths of the 1855 classification of Médoc wines in the commune of Pauillac. The name comes originally from a medieval riverside fortress whose only remains are a small round tower in the vineyard. It is now owned by an English group. Sometimes good when other vintages are 'off'.

Lebanon

One enterprising and courageous man makes the reputation of the Lebanon at Château Musar. Western European grape varieties are grown; the red is a blend of Cabernet Sauvignon, Cinsault and Syrah, aged in oak and long-lasting.

Lees

The sediment from young wine, left at the bottom of wine casks before bottling. When the wine is transferred from one keg to another (racked) the wine is gradually removed from the sediment. A wine that is bottled *sur lie* means that it comes directly from the cask, having been in contact with the lees until bottling. It should be fresher and more flavourful as a result.

Liebfraumilch

A blended wine that can only be made from white wine grapes like Riesling, Sylvaner and Müller-Thurgau, from any of four German wine regions (Rheingau, Nahe, Rheinhessen and Palatinate). Legally, Liebfraumilch must be 'mild' and, because it happens to meet the requirements, can now call itself *Qualitätswein*. It is gentle and slightly sweet.

Liquor

Wine, being an alcoholic drink is a liquor. Oliver Goldsmith, an eighteenth-century fan, said: 'Good liquor, I stoutly maintain, gives genius a better discerning.'

Loire

Regions along the banks of the châteaux-strewn, 965-kilometre (600-mile) Loire river, where some of France's best white wines are made. It divides into three main wine areas: Muscadet, Anjou-Saumur and Touraine, that stretch from the east near the mouth of the Loire river, where it empties into the Atlantic, to where it bends south after Tours; and a smaller region up in the hills south-east of Orléans, where Pouilly-Fumé and Sancerre are made. Wines to keep an eye out for are Muscadet, Anjou, Saumur, Vouvray, Touraine, Sancerre, Pouilly-Fumé and Quincy. The best wines of Anjou are blondes and sweet, and Pouilly-sur-Loire favours blondes too, but these are dry. I favour Pouilly (Fumé, that is. Pouilly-Fuissé comes from Burgundy). The best of Touraine are redheads, Chinon and Bourgueil. Rabelais was a great fan of Chinon wine, which he drank cool, even in his day.

Mâcon

The area in southern Burgundy surrounding the town of the same name (pronounced with a hard 'c', *Makon*) and the wine made there. Mâcon Villages indicates higher quality white Burgundies from specified communities in the area. Mâcons themselves can be red, pink or white but Mâcon Blanc, the most popular, is made almost exclusively from Chardonnay grapes. Pouilly-Fuissé is the best-known white appellation Mâcon. Mâcon Blanc comes from the area north of Mâcon town and is less costly, dry, very drinkable but less fine.

Madeira

Fortified wines, and the longest-lived wines in the world, from the Portuguese island of Madeira. Wines can range from very dry to very sweet, and both quality and price vary enormously. The finest, in my opinion, are Sercial (the driest), Bual and Malmsey. The latter, deep-golden and very sweet, is a marvellous dessert wine.

The island of Madeira was claimed for Portugal by Henry the Navigator in 1418. The vine was not seriously cultivated there, however, until the sixteenth century.

The distinctive flavour comes from the process of heating the wine in an *estufa*, or stove, for up to six months – an imitation of the long sea voyages to India when wine from Madeira was used as ballast and found to be considerably improved after two crossings of the Equator. In the eighteenth century Madeira rivalled Port in popularity, especially in the USA.

Maderized

When a very old wine becomes oxidized, turns brown, looks like Madeira and tastes flat, it is said to have been 'maderized'.

Madiran

Madiran is a full-bodied, dark-red wine from south-west France. Before *appellation contrôlée* it used to be shipped to Bordeaux for blending with Clarets.

Málaga

Sweet, dark, fortified wine from vineyards near the city of Málaga in southern Spain. Aged and blended in *soleras*, as is Sherry, it is actually more similar to tawny Port in flavour.

Malmsey

A king of the Madeira family of dessert wines (see also Madeira).

Manzanilla

A very light, dry Sherry made in and around the town of Sanlúcar de Barrameda near Jerez in Spain. Very pale and faintly bitter, it is the wine of bullfighters and the *tapa* bars in Spain. It is the vinous equivalent of the Dry Martini and makes a wonderful apéritif.

Margaux

Margaux is a village which gives its name to the wine commune of Margaux, one of only six in the Médoc with its own *appellation contrôlée*, and to Château Margaux, which was awarded first growth status in the famous 1855 classification.

Madame Dubarry used to send her coach 800 kilometres (500 miles) from Versailles to pick up her supplies of this magnificent Bordeaux château wine. It now belongs to a French supermarket group, Félix Potin (though not often sold in them!), whose late chief was a Greek millionaire.

Marsala

Lord Nelson used Marsala to help keep his sailors' courage high. Like Port, it was invented by Englishmen and produced, as it still is, in Sicily, by the *solera* system. It is a dry-sweet wine used as an apéritif or as a dessert drink. (Today, Marsala is made by a subsidiary of the Fiat automobile firm!)

May wine (mai wein)

More of a German rite than a drink, perhaps the predecessor of Beaujolais Nouveau. It is a new wine, flavoured with woodruff and served usually with strawberries floating in it.

Measurements

Most wines are usually measured in metric terms these days. Pressings, harvests and storage quantities are counted in hectolitres (100 litres/22 imperial gallons/26 US gallons). Some old and extremely variable names show up in books. A butt is 490 litres (108 imperial gallons) if it contains Sherry or Málaga, 572 litres (126 gallons) if it has anything else in it. A pipe holds about 523 litres (115 gallons), or two hogsheads of Port. A keg is a small cask of 45 litres (ten gallons). A barrel holds 182 litres (40 gallons). A hogshead is anything from 204 to 400 litres (45 to 88 gallons). A puncheon (usually for rum) holds 423 to 518 litres (93 to 114 gallons). For home use 16 tablespoons equal one cup and one-third of a teaspoon equals a dash!

All of the old measurements for casks are approximate, and can change according to what wine is put in them and what country they were made in. All old barrels used to be made by hand and were not a bit accurate as to content.

Médoc

The biggest and most prestigious of Bordeaux's fine wine districts. It is also the appellation for some of the more ordinary red wines produced there. Haut-Médoc wines are generally better than Médoc wines. (See also Bordeaux.)

Méthode champenoise

The process invented in, and used for making, Champagne, whereby wine undergoes a second fermentation in the bottle and thus acquires the gas that produces its sparkle. Also used for other types of sparkling wine the world over.

Minervois

Old southern French wine area (part of Languedoc-Roussillon, near Narbonne and the Mediterranean) with its own VDQS. The wine is an agreeable, flavourful red. Today it is made mainly by co-operative wine producers.

Monbazillac

Sweet white wine from near Cyrano's home, Bergerac, in south-west France. It can be luscious as an apéritif, and is equally good with cheese.

Montepulciano

Vino Nobile di Montepulciano is a wine that the Italians consider one of their best. It comes from just outside the delimited area for Chianti near Siena. A DOCG wine, it is dry and tannic, something like a fine Bordeaux, and a 'nose' like violets, they say. It lives long; a traditionally made wine.

Montilla

A delicate, straw-coloured wine from near Córdoba in Spain. It has a dry, nutty flavour. Since it is not fortified, although it is similar in taste to Sherry, it does not live long once you draw the cork.

Montrachet

The most famous *grand cru* white Burgundy. Among the best of all dry white wines, made in very small quantities (some 27,000 litres/6,000 gallons a year) in the Côte de Beaune. The vineyard is less than eight hectares (20 acres) and divided between Puligny and Chassagne. Chardonnay grapes are used, giving a pale, greeny-gold, highly alcoholic wine.

Mosel-Saar-Ruwer

One of the 11 'designated regions', or *anbaugebiete*, of German wine. Some vineyards grow on very steep slopes and two-thirds are planted with Riesling. Fresh, fruity wine.

Moselle

Moselle (Mosel in Germany) is a lighter, crisper white wine than its nearby rivals, the Rhine wines. It is made along the steep sides of the River Moselle, which rises in France but flows into Germany and empties into the Rhine. It is a delicate, elegant wine at its best.

Mousseux

French for 'frothy'. Used for any sparkling wine that is not Champagne, and for *cuve close* fizz. Sparkling wines made in Alsace and along the Loire are often called *crémant*.

Mouton-Rothschild, Château

A second growth in the 1855 vineyard classification of Médoc wines, promoted to a first growth with the 1973 vintage, thanks to the efforts of Baron Philippe de Rothschild.

Muscadet

A very agreeable white wine, popular with seafood. It is made along the Loire where it empties into the Atlantic. Since World War II it has been much in demand in France.

Musigny

One of the greatest of red Burgundies. It comes from a tiny slope in the Côte de Nuits. A delicate wine, often described as 'feminine', it is almost the equal of Romanée-Conti.

Must

The juice of the grapes, or the crushed grapes themselves, in the process of being turned into wine.

Nahe

One of Germany's 11 quality wine regions, in which Bad Kreuznach and Schloss Böckelheim are the best-known villages. Crisp, fruity wines made from Riesling, Sylvaner and Müller-Thurgau grapes.

Napa Valley

The name of a quietly pretty vineyard area north-east of San Francisco in the USA (*napa* means 'plenty' in American-Indian). It has had an enormous influence for its youth and size on the world's wine-making. It is a region of low hills and vineyards growing mainly in the flat valley, one after the other, like beads strung along the central road. Napa Valley vintners are noted for their experimenting and their care for the technical aspects of wine-making. Napa makes some of the finest red and white wines in the USA.

Twice as much red wine is produced as white, with Cabernet Sauvignon as the principal grape. Some of the valley's best-known wineries are Christian Brothers, Robert Mondavi, Sterling Vineyards, Joseph Heitz, Beaulieu Vineyards and Schramsberg. Several vineyards are now owned by European investors, including Nestlé and Moët-Hennessy. Others are owned by big American groups, such as National Distillers and Seagrams, but many are 'boutique' wineries. (See also USA; California.)

Nederburg

A famous name in South Africa for fine white wines. Nederburg Steen is crisp, slightly like Vouvray, and ages well. The vineyards are near Paarl (q.v.).

Négociant

French for a merchant who not only buys and sells wine but also handles it until it is ready to drink. Sometimes called *négociant-éleveur* – one who 'raises' the wine.

Neuchâtel

One of Switzerland's pleasant, light white wines and quite

good reds, produced on the shores of Lake Neuchâtel near the French frontier. Whites are good with lake fish.

New York State

The second largest producing area for wines in the US, with over 4,000 hectares (10,000 acres) under cultivation. Taylor Wines, Pleasant Valley Wine, Great Western sparkling wines and Walter S. Taylor (grandson of the founder of Taylor Wines) are among the best-known brands.

Nierstein

Because of new German wine rules, a huge *Bereich*, or subregion, in Germany's Rheinhessen *Anbaugebiet*, with 11 very large vineyards and 175 smaller single vineyards, is now allowed to call its wine Bereich Nierstein. 'Niersteiner Gutes Domtal' is a *Grosslage* within the *Bereich*, with some 30 vineyards which can use that appellation.

The best Niersteiner comes from the village of Nierstein and is made of Riesling grapes. So, for quality wine, look for the word Riesling, plus the name of a ranking vineyard (Hölle, Hipping, Kransberg, Orbel, etc.) on the label. These can make really noble drinking.

Noble rot

Not someone talking high-falutin' foolishness, but a type of furry mould that appears on the skins of ripening grapes

(*Botrytis cinerea* in Latin, *pourriture noble* in French and E*delfäule* in German). Far from being a pest, this rot is beneficial because it causes the natural sugar and the flavour in the berries to concentrate. If it happens before the grapes are ripe, however, this same mould is a disaster and is called 'grey rot'. Noble rot occurs especially in Sauternes in the Bordeaux area, and along the Rhine and Mosel in Germany. It also happens in Hungary for Tokay, and in California, but has not yet been much exploited in the USA.

Grapes with noble rot smell pleasant. Those with grey rot stink.

Non-vintage

Table wines are no longer allowed to use vintage dates on their labels according to the EEC rules. About the only fine non-vintage wine is French Champagne, which, in non-vintage form, being a blend, is nevertheless excellent (and less costly).

Nose

See Bouquet.

Nuits-St-Georges

Excellent red wines (and some white) made around the town of the same name on the Côte de Nuits. Typical of great Burgundies.

Oenology

Simply means the scientific study of wine. The word comes from the ancient Greek for wine (*oino*) and its word for making speeches (though *krassi* is modern Greek for wine). You can be an oenophile (lover of wine) to such a degree that you get oenomania or the DTs. But I hope not.

I have heard that André Simon, a real wine expert, was given a glass from each of two bottles of different vintages of the same wine. Simply by sniffing, he is said to have named the wine, guessed the probable vintage date of each, given all sorts of information about where the vineyards were, the rainfall of those years and the size of the crop. 'But wait, there's more,' he said, 'I'll let them breathe.' After a while he went back to the glasses, sipped them, and then said: 'This one is '72 [1872, in his case] and that one is '78.' André Simon was not an oenologist but he certainly knew as much as most of them.

Oloroso

A Spanish name for a Sherry that 'smells good'. It is darker than a *fino* and made without the 'flor' of most other Sherries. Soft, with a pronounced bouquet, it is naturally dry, but for some markets is sweetened to suit local tastes.

Orvieto

At about the knee of Italy's boot, in Umbria, the vines produce this white DOC wine from rocky volcanic soil.

One medieval artist's contract for covering Orvieto's cathedral walls with murals was cancelled because he used 'too much blue, too much gold, and too much wine'. Today, Orvieto wine is dry (or slightly sweet) and fresh with a smooth, light character.

Oxidized

Sometimes a cork may not fit tightly enough or becomes faulty, thus allowing air into a corked bottle. When this happens, oxygen spoils the wine, causing it to darken and lose palatability or even to turn into vinegar. It becomes oxidized. This seldom occurs if a wine is properly stored.

made. The area boasts a beautiful wine museum, housed in the thirteenth-century palace of the Kings of Aragon.

Pétrus

Château Pétrus is the best, and most expensive, wine of Pomerol in the Bordeaux area. Exotic, generous and full, it deserves to be counted with the *premiers crus classés*, though, like all the Pomerols, it is not officially classified. The vineyard is small, a little more than 11 hectares (28 acres). A sip or two of Château Pétrus (Peter) can certainly be heavenly, though no one seems to know why or how the vineyard came to be named after the Prince of the Apostles.

Phylloxera

A tiny plant louse that nearly brought about the annihilation of Europe's vineyards in the 1880s. Disaster was finally averted when it was discovered that European vines could be grafted onto imported American roots that were resistant to the beast.

Piemonte (Piedmont)

A most important quality wine region near Turin in Italy. Among its fine Italian wines are Barolo, Barbera and Barbaresco, along with other big, strong reds. It is also the centre for Italian sparkling wines like Asti Spumante.

Piesport

A German village famous for fruity, fragrant wines, the 'Queens of the Moselle'. Best include Goldtröpfchen, Günterslay, Domherr and Falkenberg.

Pink Champagne

French Champagne makers consider their pink version as something of a sideline, and not as interesting as their white type. Nevertheless, Moët et Chandon has a pink Dom Pérignon, their most exclusive label, and are very proud of it, and Krug has followed suit with Krug rosé. (See also Rosé.)

Plonk

An expressive term used in Britain for ordinary table wine.

Port

The world's best-known and favourite fortified wine and post-prandial potion. Its vineyards are up the Douro river from the city of Oporto in Portugal. The raw wine is shipped down to the 'big city', where it is siphoned off into casks and grape brandy is added in order to arrest fermentation. Depending on the quantity of sugar in it, the quality and sweetness of the grapes used, the cellar care it is given and the length of time it ages, the wine becomes Port (or Porto in the USA). It has a strength of about 20 per cent alcohol. Although Port is one of England's traditional drinks, the French are consuming more of it than anyone today. They use it as an apéritif.

Port has several grades of quality. The oldest can last 50 years or more. The most costly old version is Vintage Port, made from selected lots of wine in especially good years. This happens rarely, only about three times a decade. Old Tawny is a blend of old wines (ten to 40 years), and comes next in price and the esteem of fans. Plain Tawny is a blend of comparatively young wine, both red and white, to make it look something like Old Tawny. Ruby, the cheapest version, is made from young wine that has been in wooden casks for a mere two or three years.

White port is made from white grapes treated in the same way as the red, but usually drunk as an apéritif.

Pouilly-Fuissé

Famed and beautiful, dry, greeny-gold, fruity white wine made of Chardonnay grapes near Mâcon in Burgundy. It is almost a 'great wine'. At least Louis XIV thought it was great – he loved it! It should be drunk young, under three years.

Pouilly-Fuissé's vines grow at the bottom of a cliff over which, in prehistoric times, cavemen used to drive horses to their death for their own food supply. These ancient bones provide the marvellous calcium subsoil that nourishes the Pouilly-Fuissé vines.

Pouilly-Fumé

Not to be confused with Pouilly-Fuissé for it is a lesser, though still excellent, wine. It comes from the Loire valley and is dry with a smoky flavour (hence Fumé), made from Sauvignon Blanc grapes. (It might help to remember which is which to note that Fuissé and Burgundy, two longish words, go together. Fumé and Loire, two shortish ones, do likewise.)

Pourriture noble

See Noble rot.

Prädikat

See German labelling regulations.

QbA (Qualitätswein bestimmter Anbaugebiete)

See German labelling regulations.

QmP (Qualitätswein mit Prädikat)

See German labelling regulations.

Quarts de Chaume

A small but prestigious vineyard of Anjou, France, in the Coteaux du Layon. It produces a very fine, expensive, fruity, rich dessert wine.

Quinta

The Portuguese name for a farming estate. It also applies to a large vineyard.

Racking

The process of syphoning the wine from one cask or vat into a fresh one to separate the wine from its sediment or lees. This method is used for all well-made wines at least twice before they are bottled.

Retsina

An 'addictive' Greek (predominantly white) wine made, since the days of Odysseus and Achilles, with a touch of resin. It is an acquired taste but once acquired the wine can be delicious, chilled, to accompany an outdoor meal. Half of Greece's wine consumption is of retsina.

Rheingau

One of the 11 regions for quality wine in Germany. This is the perfect Riesling region, on the right bank of the Rhine between Rüdesheim and Mainz, famous for quality since the days of Charlemagne. Its star vineyard and wine is Johannisberg. Wines are elegant, spicy and fruity. The greatest of German wine areas.

Rheinhessen

A major member of the 11 demarcated wine regions of Germany on the left bank of the Rhine. Riesling vines got their name in 1404 and are still grown here, along with others. The area makes mainly soft aromatic white wines, using largely Sylvaner grapes.

Rheinpfalz

See Palatinate.

Rioja

Rioja is probably the best name in Spanish wine. It is produced in a picturesque Shangri-La-like area between two mountain ranges at the upper end of the steep Ebro River valley, some 60 miles south-east of Bilbao in the Basque country. It is divided into three regions: the Rioja Alta, Rioja

Alavesa and Rioja Baja. The Rioja Alta, which is the farthest west, and the Rioja Alavesa, north of the Ebro, both produce fine, elegant wines. To the east, the Rioja Baja in lower, flatter, hotter terrain, produces a more Mediterranean type of less acid, stronger wine, used for blending.

The area was making wine in Roman days. It got a special boost when French vintners moved to Spain in the 1870s and '80s to escape the devastation of the phylloxera bug in their own country, bringing Bordeaux methods with them. Today's Rioja wines reflect this influence in their oakiness. Some of the Rioja's giant new wine factories look like sets from Hollywood futuristic films, using automated modern methods of vinification and production, epoxy-lined steel tanks, and all. Other smaller bodegas, like Muga, maintain the style of the past, making wine in small quantities, ageing in oak, racking twice a year, and producing big, robust, characterful wines. Still other producers are making Riojas with no time spent in wood, known as *rioja sin crianza*.

Rioja is noted especially for its reds (mostly blended), some of which can give Bordeaux a run for its money. The Spaniards tend to keep wine longer in barrels than the French do today. But the aristocrats of Rioja, its *reserva* and *gran reserva* wines, are 'noble' vintage-labelled wines with a delicate bouquet and a roundness of flavour that can last up to a quarter of a century, continuing to grow in quality. They are also excellent value.

Rioja has a peculiar labelling system. Wines are marked 2° Año, or 3° Año, indicating the wine was bottled two or three years after harvesting. Some *reservas*, however, are given true vintage dates. Sometimes a back label indicates length of ageing. A wine marked *crianza* (educated) is bottled in the third year after harvest. *Reservas* (red) spend much more time in wood, giving them lightness and fragrance despite being four or more years old. *Gran reservas* are

usually eight years old, and can be majestic. The recent trend for white Riojas is to keep them for shorter periods in wood, producing a nice, dry, fruity, fresh wine.

Some of the best producers include: Bodegas Frederico Paternina, Viños de las Herederos del Marqués de Riscal, Bodegas Marqués de Murrieta, Bodegas Franco Españolas, Bodegas La Rioja Alta, Bodegas Lan, Bodegas Olarra, Bodegas Marqués de Cáceres, Bodegas Alavesas, Bodegas Faustino Martinez, Lopez R. de Heredia, Bodegas Berberana, Bodegas Muga.

Rites

Wine attracts ceremony like no other form of food or drink. These mysterious rites, holdovers from bygone days, can still amuse aficionados. Among the most common is the British custom of 'passing the Port', which must be done from right to left, else you risk dire unnamed consequences. Apparently it was instituted because, while so doing with your right hand, it was difficult to whip out your sword surreptitiously to stab your neighbour withal.

The Greeks played a fine unisex game at feasts, called *kollotos*. Anyone who was not comatose would toss the last remaining drips of wine from his (or her) glass into a brass dish that was balanced on the point of a spear. The one who upset the dish had to buy a round of drinks.

Another Greek idea was to ask guests to propose a toast to their mistresses. Anyone who would not or could not had to spell her name out, drinking a cup of wine with each letter. (Hard luck on anyone whose girlfriend was Clytemnestra.)

More recently, in northern Europe at the end of a banquet, an enormous goblet called a Constable, filled with wine, was put on the table. Anyone who did not keep up with the crowd, cup for cup, was forced to drink the entire Constable-ful.

Ostentatiously, in rich houses, when glass was rare and costly, guests would throw their glasses over their shoulder when empty. Inflation probably stopped that rite.

Today Scandinavians must toast each other with a *skoal*, after which they drink, gazing into each other's eyes. Strangely the Chinese also toast before drinking. The host has to give the signal, or no one can take a sip of rice wine.

Romanée-Conti

Tops in red Burgundies. The Prince de Conti, who owned it from 1760 to 1795, was an ancestor of one of today's two owners, Madame Bize-Leroy and Hubert de Villaine, energetic forces in the wine world. It is a tiny two-hectare (5-acre) plot in Vosne-Romanée, producing only about 600 cases of wine a year.

Romania

Romania comes sixth in world wine production but little of it is seen in the West. Romania follows the Russian preference for heavy, sweet wine.

Rosé

Pink wine whose colour is obtained either by colouring a white wine with cochineal, mixing red and white wines, or using ripe red grapes and leaving the skins in the freshly pressed juice (or must) only long enough to tint the wine but not during fermentation. The last way is the only method considered to be 'cricket'. The best rosés are Tavel, Anjou and some from California.

Rosé d'Anjou

Usually a sound, inexpensive, light pink wine for carafe or table use. Some good ones are made around Champigny on the lower Loire.

Rotwein

Red wine, in German.

Roussillon

See Languedoc-Roussillon.

Rüdesheim

A superior German wine-producing village in the Rheingau.
Its vineyards are very steep and planted with Riesling
grapes. Its wines are distinguished, full-bodied and
outstanding. (There is another Rüdesheim in the Nahe, not
anywhere near as great, but its labels must state Nahe; so
watch for the word Rheingau when buying.)

Russia

Although most Westerners have never even seen a Russian
wine, to say nothing of tasting it, Russia is the world's third
largest wine-producing nation after Italy and France.
Russian wines are made for the Russian taste, naturally,
which means that three-quarters of them are very sweet,
often containing about as much sugar as alcohol.

Most of their wine is consumed in Russia, but some 73
million litres (16 million gallons) of it are exported. Red,
white, rosé and sparkling wines are made. The largest
quantity comes from the southern coast of Russia along the
Black Sea. Wines from the Crimea are probably the best,
especially a Madeira-type 'Muscatel'. Other areas are south
of the Sea of Azov, Armenia, Georgia and Moldavia, which
used to be part of Romania. 'Champanski' is made to the
tune of 100 million bottles a year.

Ruwer

One of three areas that form the 'designated region' of
Mosel-Saar-Ruwer in Germany, which is the wording its
labels carry. The Ruwer itself is a wee tributary of the Mosel
and its own wee valley. Its best Riesling wines are superb,
growing on some of the steepest land in Germany, cliffs of
black slate facing south.

Saar

Another tributary of the Mosel. Many of Germany's Saar river banks are like cliffs, terraced to keep the soil from sliding down into the river. Yet from them comes a great deal of delicious Mosel wine mainly made from Riesling grapes – fresh, steely, austere, but low in alcohol and marvellous for summer sipping. Of German wines, Mosel is my favourite.

Sack

The old English name for Sherry. Its derivation is probably from the Spanish word *sacar* (to export), for a great deal of it was shipped out of Spain to Britain. Shakespeare's Falstaff was one of its early aficionados. In those days it was a rather sweet wine (as is its modern namesake 'Dry Sack', despite the adjective).

Sir Francis Drake, among other more adventuresome exploits, 'liberated' some 2,900 pipes of it (that's over 1.5 million litres, or 330,000 gallons!) from Cádiz when he raided the place in 1587, and shipped it back to England. Dr Samuel Johnson used to take on quantities of Sack, stumble home to sleep and sweat it off, then fall to studying.

Saint Émilion

One of the really fine red wine-producing regions of Bordeaux. The area, east of Bordeaux itself, has a cosier feeling than the Médoc, with small farms and few imposing châteaux. The appellation area is divided into the hilly Côtes vineyards where most of the best wines are, around the town of Saint Émilion, and the plateau nearer the Dordogne with gravelly terrain. The Côtes' top wine is Château Ausone; the flatter part boasts Cheval Blanc. Both are *premier grand cru classé* and jointly head the list of 12 such for Saint Émilion, though Château Figeac is close behind. Merlot and Cabernet grapes are used mainly. The best of its wines keep well and are fruity and rich with a heady aroma.

Saint Estèphe

Main township of the Haut-Médoc with some fine châteaux,

such as Calon-Ségur, Cos-d'Estournel and Montrose among the best, while some of the bourgeois growths, like Phélan-Ségur, run them a close second. Full-bodied, generous wines in general. The commune of Saint Estèphe has its own *appellation contrôlée*.

Saint Julien

The heart of the Haut-Médoc with some excellent wines, though none are first growths. Don't let that put you off, however, for you can hardly go wrong with Beychevelle, Ducru-Beaucaillou, Talbot and any of those starting with 'Léoville'. The plain appellation, Saint Julien, is usually the most expensive of Bordeaux regional wines.

Saint Vincent

The patron saint of wine, especially in France, though he was a Spaniard and there are no records of his ever having drunk wine at all. The Burgundians claim he got the job because of his name – *Vin-cent*.

Sancerre

Pale, fresh white wine from around the town of Sancerre in the upper part of the Loire valley and made exclusively from Sauvignon grapes. A very agreeable summer drinking wine, popular in France. Its name comes from the Latin name for the town, *Castellum Sancti Satyri*, 'the castle of the holy satyrs'.

Saumur

This region produces some of the Loire's best wines, and is still small enough for you to visit its producers and chat with them while you taste their wares, usually in the kitchen of their farmhouse. The views along the river are gentle rather than spectacular.

Saumur is best known for its range of sparkling wines, made for decades by the same methods as Champagne. Its original vintners emigrated from Champagne in the nineteenth century, bringing their skills with them. Sparkling Saumur (Crémant de la Loire) is among the best of non-Champagne sparkling wines.

For those who can find it, still Saumur is also a most palatable dry white wine that lives long and will improve in the bottle. Saumur makes rosé and red wines too, both still and sparkling, but its whites are superior.

Sauternes

(Spelt with a final 's' in both singular and plural.) Along with Barsac, which is next door, Sauternes lies about 48 kilometres (30 miles) south of Bordeaux, tucked into but not part of the general appellation of Graves. Sauternes is the home of Château d'Yquem, perhaps the most famous and costliest white wine in the world. That is the summit of the region's range of wines, but there are many marvellous dessert wines (Château La Tour Blanche, for example) at lower levels.

Sauternes lasts for a very long time. It is made from Sémillon and Sauvignon Blanc grapes that are allowed to become overripe. With luck, they will then be attacked by 'noble rot', which, when the weather is right, concentrates even further the sugar content of the grapes and can then produce a special-tasting, sweet (but not sickly sweet), luscious elixir fit for gods.

Today, however, when conditions are not right for making the best of sweet, the must from the area may sometimes be turned into dry appellation Bordeaux Blanc. Of course this wine cannot be sold as Sauternes, but it comes from the same area.

In the USA, 'Sauterne' (without final 's') is used for ordinary table wine almost interchangeably with 'Chablis', and neither bears any resemblance to either original.

Savoie

Nearly all white wine, produced in alpine conditions from local grape varieties. Best known are Crépy, which is still, and Seyssel, which is often sparkling, and also Apremont.

Schaumwein

German for sparkling wines in general.

Schools of wine

Many wine schools have sprung up in recent years. Among those worth joining as a student are: Académie du Vin (Paris); Université du Vin (Drôme, France); German Wine Academy (Wiesbaden, Germany); École du Vin (Château Loudenne, France); Wine and Spirit Education Trust, for professionals (London); Christie's Wine Course (London); Académie du Vin (New York).

The University of California has a College of Agriculture with an oenological department at the town of Davis, north of San Francisco. It has played a very large part in the world's switch from 'rule of thumb' viticulture to the new scientific approach to wine-making. Its influence is strong in the USA and has made a great impression on Europe, Australia and South Africa as well.

The London Guildhall Library, although not a school, has a unique collection of books, periodicals and maps dealing with wine.

Sekt

German term for the better grades of sparkling wine. It started as the German equivalent of British 'Sack' for Sherry. However, a famous German actor, playing Falstaff in the last century, used the term even when ordering his true favourite, Champagne, in bars and restaurants. The idea took on with his public, and has become part of the German language ever since.

Sercial

The grape used for a type of Madeira wine, the driest of them, which is also called Sercial. Best used as an apéritif, it should age for at least eight years before drinking.

The grapes grow on high slopes. They used to be trodden barefoot and the must then brought to Funchal (the capital of the island of Madeira) in goatskin bags, which may have accounted for their rich old-time flavour! Modernized now to being transported in flavourless trucks and to mechanical crushing, the wine is fermented completely then fortified (unlike Port and older Madeiras, whose fermentation is stopped in mid-stream, so to speak).

Shakespeare

Shakespeare knew the effects of wine, both good and bad, or at least some of his characters' remarks would so indicate. Here are a few of his pronouncements on this interesting subject:
'Good wine is a good familiar creature if it be well used.' (*Othello*)
'I have very poor and unhappy brains for drinking.' (*Othello*)
'I am falser than vows made in wine.' (*As You Like It*)
'Though I look old, I am strong and lusty,
For in my youth I never did apply
Hot and rebellious liquors in my blood.' (*As You Like It*)
'A cup of hot wine with not a drop of allaying Tiber in't.' (*Coriolanus*)
'A man cannot make him laugh, but that's no marvel
He drinks no wine!' (*King Henry IV*)
'Let my liver rather heat with wine
Than my heart cool with mortifying groans.'
(*The Merchant of Venice*).

Sherry

See Jerez.

Sicily

The home of the Mafia makes more wine than any other region of Italy.

Soave

The ubiquitous and very good Italian white wine. In vineyards near Verona its vines are trained on high trellises. Soave is light, pale in colour, fresh and smoothly dry. It is a wine that should be, and usually is, drunk before it even reaches puberty.

The name was originally that of a Barbarian tribe, the Sevi. Romans tamed these wild men so successfully that their name in its present form means 'gentle' in Italian.

Soils

You may have noticed that vines like the worst kinds of terrain. Châteauneuf-du-Pape, for instance, grows on what looks like a riverbed of very big (some over a foot across) flat round pebbles. Rhine and Mosel wines grow on slopes that are almost cliffs. Champagne and Sherry love chalk. The Médoc soil is made up of small pebbles.

Such soil does not hold water on its surface, so vine roots must dig deep to find it, going through layers of land that have different nutriments to offer them. Vines that don't struggle usually produce unexciting wines. Vines need good drainage, sunshine, but not too much of it, and protection from strong winds. They like the slopes of river banks, where the river becomes a moderator of the air's temperature.

Solera

This is the system used in Spain for making Sherry. The new wine is poured into the top layer of rows of casks, piled up three or four deep. The wine is drawn off (racked) from the topmost layer to the one below, and so on, to blend for a year or so with the ageing Sherry below it, until it eventually reaches the bottom layer. Here it is drawn off for a final blend before bottling. About one-third of the cask is taken off, thus 'racked' each time, while the rest is left to blend with the wine from above. This ensures that the character of the final blend is as uniform over the years as possible.

The system is also copied in other sherry-making countries. In California it is used for the best of its 'sherries', as it is in South Africa, which makes the best imitation 'sherry' outside of Spain.

Sommelier

The wine waiter, the man in a restaurant who should know more about wine than you do and can advise on what to drink with what. He is supposed, ideally, to know what 'crus' he has in his cellar, what the wine is like and what his vintage years are. He knows how to present the wine and how to serve it. French gourmets (in restaurants with big cellars) like to offer him a sip of the wine so he can remember its taste and check up on how it is developing. This way he can better inform his future customers about the stock.

Sonoma

From the historical (though not the commercial) viewpoint, the most important of California's wine-producing counties (and therefore of the USA's). Spaniards first brought the vine to California, but it was an adventurous Hungarian, Count Agoston Haraszthy, who originally made a success of wine-making in the Sonoma Valley on his Buena Vista estate in the 1850s. He brought thousands of cuttings of over 300 grape varieties with him, planting them experimentally.

A hundred years later, James Zellerbach, a successful businessman and diplomat, decided to apply the latest scientific methods to improving American wine-making with Clos de Vougeot and Romanée Conti as his models of quality. His research discovered the importance of malolactic fermentation, the use of cold fermentation and employment of an inert gas 'cap' to reduce wine's contact with air during handling, among other innovations.

Today the area is one of the most productive and best of Californian wine regions. Wineries there include names like Sebastiani, Buena Vista, Hanzell, Simi, Korbel, Souverain and Italian Swiss Colony. Wines from the area compete in quality with some of the best in the world.

South Africa

The heart of the South African vineyards is around the towns of Paarl and Stellenbosch. The industry is concentrated in the hands of the KWV, a sort of national co-operative with five wineries. There is a strict system to

control the origins of the wines, with 14 designated areas.

South Africa used to be known abroad for its 'port' and 'sherry', but the production of table wines, always good, has improved dramatically in recent years.

Spanish labelling regulations

Spain's wine law is controlled by a central *Instituto de Denominaciones de Origen* (INDO). The Institute's local delegates can give wines that meet various production and methodical requirements a 'Denominacion de Origen' printed on the label or, alternatively, a small map of the region (Rioja). There is no quality guarantee, however.

Reserva on a red wine label indicates that the bottle contains wine aged for at least three years in cask and bottle, including a minimum of one year in cask. Rosé and white 'reservas' must have two years in all of ageing, with six months in oak. *Gran reserva*, for reds, requires two years in cask plus three in bottle. For rosé and white wines, it shows a total of four years age with six months in cask.

Sparkling wine

The most famous is Champagne from France. The best of the rest is made by the French Champagne method (*méthode champenoise*). Others are made by the bulk process, fermented in tanks and bottled under pressure. Least good is the method of charging still wine with carbon dioxide gas, as it if were a soft drink. Sparkling wines are known as *mousseux* or *crémant* in France, *spumante* in Italy, *cava* in Spain, *sekt* in Germany. Sparkling wines, some authorities think, are 'lighter' than still ones, and less intoxicating. Some sparkling red wine is made, sparkling Burgundy being the best known.

Spätlese

The second rung of the QmP ladder of quality for German wines. It is made from grapes that are picked after the normal harvest period is over. The wine is slightly sweet. (See also German labelling regulations.)

Spirits

Wine is often converted into spirits by distilling. The most famous and perhaps best of these are the brandies, Cognac and Armagnac, both from France. Less good is Marc (pronounced *mar*) which is made from the skins and pulp of grapes left over after pressing for wine. Germany makes good brandy, often from wine they have bought from France. Italian, Spanish, Greek, American, Mexican and other brandies are made from grapes wherever they grow.

Wine is also converted into Vermouth, spiced and herbed drinks used as apéritifs, and probably the descendants of the flavoured wines the Romans used to like.

Spumante

The Italian name for sparkling wines. Their most famous version is Asti Spumante.

Stellenbosch

A beautiful, mountainous wine region of South Africa, home of Stellenbosch University, which has an oenological department. Produces excellent white wines from various white grapes and most of the country's red wines, mainly from Cabernet Sauvignon grapes. Many of South Africa's best producers have estates in this select area.

Storage

Paraphrasing what the old Spiritual says about shoes – 'Everybody talk about cellars ain't a-havin' 'em' – any collection of wines, from ten bottles to 10,000, is called a cellar these days. In cities, where people live in layers of apartments, a real cellar is an impossibility, so why not a 'wine cupboard'?

Choose a location that keeps a fairly even temperature and is not close to hot pipes. Fill it with wooden or metal racks made commercially to hold bottles. Decide what your family and your entertaining requirements are and stock up with the supply you need.

If you have a suburban house, space is not such a problem, but select a dark, dry corner away from jarring traffic and central heating. (I happen not to follow these rules, myself. My cupboard is under the stairs, which is not recommended because brooms and household equipment are stored there also. But I've never noticed that my wines, especially if they are young ones, have suffered as a result.)

You will need enough racks to keep at least four dozen bottles if you drink wine every day. However, a city apartment's maximum sensible capacity would be about a month's supply. The number of bottles will depend on the tastes, the thirsts, the entertainment lists and the purse of each individual family.

Keep a list of what you have and use, not in a cellar-book but a cupboard-book, and make notes of the wines you like, with prices, vintages and any other comments which you think might be useful for future reference. Some suppliers will keep wines in store for you if you have some fine ones you want really carefully tended.

'Company wines' (say about five per cent of the total) should be kept in reserve for entertaining special guests who might appreciate them. Wines for everyday use with meals should be those that suit your own taste. Beyond them, you can collect rare and expensive wines as you might collect books or prints. But take care (by tasting them occasionally) not to let these sit around so long that they get past the optimum age for drinking.

Sur lie

See Lees.

Switzerland

The Swiss actually import wine because their own production, though very good, is too small. Its best wines are Dôle (red), Neuchâtel (red and white) and Fendant (white). All are pleasant drinking wines, but not 'great'.

Tafelwein

See German labelling regulations.

Talbot

Bordeaux château with a British name. John Talbot was an ex-governor of Ireland, a general who, during the 100 Years War, saved Normandy for England and was given this Saint Julien vineyard as reward. Later, he lost the battle of Castillon and lost Bordeaux to the French. 'He killed more Frenchmen than the plague,' say Bordeaux vintners, 'but he taught the English princes to love French wine!' So they kept his name to identify the estate.

Tannin

That puckery sensation you have in your mouth when you taste a young red wine is tannin. It comes from grape stems and skins, and some is picked up from the wood of the oaken casks it ages in. It does not taste good in large quantities, but it is very good for the wine. It is a preservative, so the more a top-quality young wine has, the longer it will take to become fully mature, and the longer it will eventually live. Luckily for us all, the tannin taste gets less powerful with age (it is part of the sediment left in the bottle by fine red wines) so old Bordeaux, especially, has less tannin than when it is a mere youth.

Tasting

(See also Oenology and Palate.) Tasting, when it comes to wine, is a 'portmanteau' word that includes several faculties. Sip, swill, aerate, pause and spit are the five rather unattractive-sounding activities that, together with sniffing and looking, make a wine-taster, but they do not confer instant expertise.

Wine should have a 'bright' whiteness or redness or shades in between. White wine is over the hump when it is brownish. The serious taster should take note of colour, holding the wine to the light to obtain the best impression.

Red wine is purplish when young, becoming 'ruby', then red or red-brown when it is at its best. It finally becomes

lighter and browner, when it might still be great, but is likely also to have passed its prime.

The smell of wine, known as its 'nose', is described usually in very personal terms by experts – such as prune and raspberry. But white wines, especially, are definitely fruity. Some reds smell like vanilla; whites compare with flowers or honey.

Taste itself is also hard to describe, though sweetness, acidity and tannin are fairly simple to recognize. Body, if you like, is the wine's thickness. Don't dream of becoming a wine-master unless you have a top-notch taste memory. Serious tasters abhor the use of perfume and the smell of cigars and cigarettes while tasting.

Tavel

The most famous rosé of France from the southern Côtes du Rhône, powerfully alcoholic, dry, rather redder than most rosés, and eminently drinkable.

Taylor

A famous old Port house, as well as the name of the biggest American vintner outside California. The American Taylor started life in northern New York's productive Finger Lake area. Now owned by Seagrams, its Taylor California Cellars, set up only a few years ago, has become one of the half-dozen largest wine producers in that state too. In Europe the wine cannot use the word 'Taylor' because the Port firm has priority on the name, so it is sold as California Cellars.

Temperatures

White wine should be chilled, in most cases, for drinking. The best method is to use an ice-bucket or any vessel big enough to hold a bottle, covered up to its shoulder in water with a trayful of ice floating in it. If the bottle goes in the refrigerator, it should not be left too long: half an hour to an hour is enough. It should not be icy, just chilled, to get the most out of its bouquet and flavour.

As to red wines, their aroma (bouquet) and taste is more pronounced when they are warmer, around 15°C/60°F. The

old rule of thumb about room temperature is a bit vague, since some rooms are frigid, others too hot. Young red wines, like Beaujolais, are often served cool, but a fine wine should be brought to that 15°C/60°F temperature gradually, leaving it an hour or so in the dining room before drinking.

In a cellar, wine should be kept at about 10°C/50°F, so that it does not mature too rapidly. Heat tends to rush things too much. And a cellar's temperature should remain as constant as possible, free of draughts and reasonably dry. Dampness does no harm, except that the labels fall off, making it hard to tell whether you are picking out a plonk or a treasure.

Tempo

Wine is not really acclimatized to the jet age. The proper tempo for drinking it is leisurely. Its whole manufacture, with only occasional spurts of activity like harvesting, is slow. Vines take five years to become productive. Wine itself needs time to mature, sometimes as long as 50 years.

Leave hypertension to the spirits drinkers. Wine is almost meditative and its admirers enjoy it because it diffuses warmth and friendliness as nothing else can. As Brillat-Savarin said: 'Entertaining a guest means you take charge of his happiness for the whole time he is with you.' What better way to treat a guest than to drink wine together slowly, and with friends?

Tinto

Vino tinto is red wine in Spanish, and it is *vinho tinto* in Portuguese.

Tokay

Along with Château d'Yquem, this is one of the world's most celebrated white dessert wines. It comes from Hungary, and its unusual vines have grown there since before the Barbarians took over the country more than 1,000 years ago. It is 70 per cent made from a grape practically unused in other wine countries, the Furmint, and is sold in bottles about two-thirds the size of ordinary wine bottles.

Government-controlled, not much Tokay is exported these days. The best, Eszencia, is made by letting late-picked grapes' own weight squeeze out nectar-like juice. So little is produced that Eszencia is hardly ever to be found at all. Aszú is the best grade of Tokay now available, made with a kind of paste of grape berries mixed with overripe grapes, which gives the wine a most distinctive aroma and flavour. Less expensive but still good is the Szamorodni grade, generally dry.

Tokay is also used as a name applied to the Pinot Gris grape in Alsace and to a Californian grape called Flame Tokay. Neither one has anything at all to do with Hungarian Tokay wine, despite their names.

It is said that Pope Leo XIII was kept alive for the last two weeks of his 93-year-old life entirely on Eszencia.

Trockenbeerenauslese

Really three words run into one, meaning dried-berry-selection, and referring to a highly regarded German dessert wine, the top-category QmP wine. It is made by allowing the grapes to stay on the vines until they begin to dry out and their sugar content becomes concentrated as they are attacked by noble rot. They are then picked individually by hand, using only the ripest berries. This selective picking means the wines are scarce and very expensive.

Tuscany

The beautiful, hilly region around and south of Florence where Chianti is made. Some Chianti Classico is on a par with the best wines to be found anywhere.

United States of America

In the past 20 years the USA has suddenly become important as a wine-producing country. America's talent for experimenting has produced a number of new ideas about vinification and the treatment of wines. Developing grape varieties for specific climates, treating root stock with heat, machine-pickers for grapes, drip irrigation and cold fermentation are among the 'inventions' the USA has given the wine industry.

In Europe the making of wine used to be a mystery lore handed down from father to son, and was more often than not a matter of chance. The American idea was that wine-making could be made less of a gamble if scientific attention were paid to it. Technology has improved wine-making worldwide and has made it possible to mass-produce good wine.

California is where most of the USA's wine comes from, more than 85 per cent of it. The Napa Valley produces some of its best. New York State also has a lively wine industry with about ten per cent of the total. There is some wine produced in almost every state, but in very tiny quantities.

US *labelling regulations*

In California the grape variety or 'varietal' and the name of the wine-maker are more important than the origin of the grapes. There must be 75 per cent of a varietal in the wine for it to be mentioned on the label. With higher-quality wines, this is often nearer 100 per cent. California is working out a system of designated regions to include counties and smaller areas.

USSR

See Russia.

Valais

One of the best cantons for vine-growing in Switzerland. It is in the mountains near the source of the Rhône. Skiers *en route* to Montana and Zermatt pass through it. Wines made in the Valais include red Dôle and white Johannisberg and Fendant. The vines, some 3,600 hectares (9,000 acres) of them, stretch from the foot of Mont Blanc to the Simplon tunnel.

Valdepeñas

In Spain this is an easily appreciable wine, usually associated with the plains of La Mancha between Madrid and Seville, the fabled country of Don Quixote. Valdepeñas is now supposed to be called Vino de la Mancha. It is a very drinkable table wine, usually best when young. The reds are light and fresh. This one area where it is made produces more wine than the whole of California.

Valpolicella

A good, mass-produced Italian wine from the Veneto, not far from Venice and Verona. It is fruity and aromatic, light but subtle. The better grades, Valpolicella Superiore, stay in wood for about 18 months and improve in the bottle for about five years. The lighter version is made into carafe wine to be drunk young. As a carafe wine it is excellent.

In Greek, the word meant 'valley of many caves' (or cellars), implying that it was a well-known wine-producing area long before the Romans came.

Varietal

A word invented in America to describe wines made from a particular variety of grape. The term is being used not only in the USA but in newer wine-growing countries. Fortunately for all concerned, this eliminates the confusing former tendency to name unsuitable wines after traditional regional 'golden oldies'. 'Chablis', for instance, is a name taken in vain far too frequently. European wines' grape content is usually defined by law and their normally regional, or generic, names are justified by centuries of

usage. The use of generic names in California, Australia, or by other non-European wine-growers, was a way of indicating to buyers what general type of wine to expect. Sometimes this definition of a wine was very misleading.

Vaud

A Swiss canton where white wines, in the main, are grown on the lovely slopes of Lake Geneva near Lausanne. The wine is mainly Fendant (known here as Dorin) and the main grape is Chasselas. The wines are consumed almost entirely by the Swiss themselves.

VDQS (Vin Délimité de Qualité Supérieure)

See French labelling regulations.

Vendange, Vendimia, Vendemmia

The French, Spanish and Italian words respectively for the vintage, or harvest-time. (See also Vintage.)

Verdicchio

In the 'muscle' of Italy's leg, near Ancona, is the country of Verdicchio, a wine that was already popular in the days when the Goths rampaged through Italy. Alaric the Visigoth chieftain took some of it with him to help in the sack of Rome in AD 401. It comes in a waisted bottle, supposed to be like the *amphora* in which the Romans used to sell it. Despite its bottle, it is a sound, unpretentious, pale, fresh wine. Being white, it goes well with fish and white meats.

Vernaccia di San Gimignano

This DOC wine comes from San Gimignano, near Siena. One of the 'divine' Tuscan wines, it was said to be Michaelangelo's favourite. Pale golden, fresh, dry and elegant as a table wine today, it used to be sweet and dark for a white wine, almost like Sherry. San Gimignano, by the way, is an interesting town to visit. Its groups of square watch-towers give the impression of a medieval preview of the skyscraper cities of today.

Vin doux naturel

A sweet wine made by adding wine brandy to wine to stop its fermentation. This ensures that it will have a high sugar content and thus high alcoholic strength. Mostly sold in France as an apéritif.

Vin de paille

Literally 'straw wine', a yellowish wine so called because of its colour and because the grapes used for it are laid out on beds of straw to dry out before being pressed. It is a sweet and long-lived wine, mainly produced in the Jura region of France.

Vin de pays

The next step up from *vin de table* in the grading of French wines. (See also French labelling regulations.)

Vin de table

The lowest rung of the French wine category ladder. (See also French labelling regulations.)

Vines

See Grape varieties.

Vinho verde

Portuguese 'green wine', so called not because of its colour but because it is made from unripe grapes grown on high trellises in the north of the country. It is slightly sparkling, or *pétillant*, leaving a prickly sensation on the tongue, very fresh and dry. It is the perfect summer drink when chilled. My favourite kind is Gatão, with a Puss-in-Boots on its label, but Aveleda is another fine example.

Vino

The same word is used by both Italians and Spaniards to mean wine. Vinho (*veenyo*), is the Portuguese word for it.

Vintage

For fine wines vintage dates are very important because the personality of the wine can vary from year to year, depending on weather conditions and, of course, on how well each wine ages. As wines age, their characteristics change too. To be able to keep track of all this takes more time and patience and a better memory than most of us have. Thus a vintage chart can be a useful gadget to invest in, especially if you intend to have an active restaurant life or to drink a good deal of fine wine. For average, day-to-day drinking, vintages play a fairly small part.

Most wines sold these days really should be drunk by the time they are from three to five years old. The exceptions are the *crus classés* of Bordeaux, the powerful Burgundies and some of the best of the Italian and Spanish red wines. As to white wines, all but the costliest of Burgundies, the superb sweet dessert wines of Bordeaux, the German late-picked ones and Tokays can be drunk almost immediately.

Virgil

The old Latin poet's name may seem a strange one to appear in a wine book, but he was a master of wine in his time. In his discursive poem *The Georgics* he wrote about the making of wine in what seem almost modern terms.

He recommended planting vines as far apart from each other as the width of a horse's hind quarters, to let them pass along the rows. Today's are planted wide enough apart to let a tractor in between.

He was an experimenter: 'Look with favour on a bold

beginning,' he said. He also knew that closely packed earth was favourable to healthy vines, while loosely packed soil was better for grains. 'Inspect the place in advance,' he advised, and went on to recommend: 'Admire a large estate, but work a small one!' and that, 'Southern heights will yield hardy vineyards full of wine. Your vine slopes must avoid the setting sun.'

Virgil also very sensibly remarked that, 'Unless your hoe attacks the weed unceasingly; unless you chase off thieving birds with frightful shout, and prune away the shady, darkening growth; unless you pray for rain in helpless want, you'll gaze upon a neighbour's teaming store, and soothe your thirst with forest acorns!'

Viticulture

The science and art of cultivating the vine and growing grapes. Often confused with vinification, which is the science of wine production, including the preparation and fermentation of the grapes.

Volnay

A wine of the Côte de Beaune with a strong bouquet; and the name of the village where its vines grow. It is one of the most agreeable of the Beaune wines. The red wine is soft and velvety, and in good years ranks with the top wines in Burgundy. The Latins used to say (at risk of being misinterpreted in modern terms) that 'you can't be gay without drinking Volnay'.

Vougeot

Vougeot is a commune in Burgundy whose *grand cru*, Clos de Vougeot, comes from a vineyard that makes about five times as much wine as the rest of the commune's vineyards put together. The Clos itself is a walled manor and a former monastery of the Cistercian order of monks founded in the twelfth century. Today it has more than 80 owners, with a consequent variety of qualities of wine.

The best of Vougeot is a big, rich wine with a complex nose. The *Confrérie des Chevaliers du Tastevin*, the brotherhood of Burgundy wines, holds its meetings in the Clos.

Wein

German word for wine.

Weingut

A German vineyard property, including its wines, cellars, the winery and all its trappings.

Wine

Wine is probably the only liquid that is more sought after than Middle East oil, and a good deal more palatable – though, weight for weight, equally a good deal more costly. Wine is the pressed and fermented juice of the fruit of the vine.

Wine is not just a beverage, unlike most other drinks it is a living thing and an inspiration for poets. Homer, puzzlingly, described the sea as being 'wine-dark'. G. K. Chesterton claimed that, 'The wine they drink in Paradise They make in Haute Lorraine.' The Church uses wine in one of its sacraments. The Bible makes frequent mention of wine. Luther, of all people, is supposed to have written, 'Who loves not woman, wine and song/Remains a fool his whole life long.'

My battered copy of *Bartlett's Quotations* lists over 100 references to wine, and even that is probably only a tiny percentage of all there are.

Wine excesses

André Simon has written that wine's excesses 'cannot be gauged in terms of quantity. There are people who can drink a bottle of Claret with pleasure and profit and yet may be seriously indisposed if they drink a second glass of Port. Others will enjoy a bottle after dinner and yet cannot drink a glass of Claret without suffering heartburn. Neither could be counted among the average drinkers. The average wine drinker would be likely to consider anything over a bottle a day as excess.'

On the other hand, an American wine expert, Richardson Wright, who certainly must have been less abstemious than he sounds, wrote that 'six is the number |of dinner guests| to choose for a single bottle of wine'. I'm afraid I would lose most of my friends if I treated them in so miserly a fashion. I consider half a bottle per person to be a minimum.

Wine Lake

(See also Languedoc-Roussillon.) Although 'Wine Lake' is the appropriately liquid way some refer to the oceans of ordinary wine that flow from one of the world's most productive wine areas, the Languedoc-Roussillon in southern France, the biggest real wine lake ever must have been the one ordered by the then Admiral of the Fleet, Sir Edward Russell, for a party on 25th October, 1695. He was entertaining 6,000 close friends, so he put the fountain of his estate to work.

His staff filled the fountain with four barrels of *eau-de-vie*, eight of clarified water, 25,000 lemons, 40 quarts of lemon juice, 1,300 pounds of sugar (he had a sweet tooth), five pounds of grated nutmeg, 300 crumbled biscuits for body and, last but not least, a pipe (about 568 litres/125 gallons) of Málaga wine.

To serve his 6,000 guests, he had a 12-year-old boy, an apprentice sailor, elegantly dressed, rowing around this 'lake' in a specially built rosewood boat, dipping out portions to all and sundry. There is no record of what the assembled multitude thought about the wine lake's aroma and flavour, but there is little doubt that it was spectacular.

Xeres

Xeres is the name the Romans gave to what is now Jerez in Spain, the home of Sherry. The word is still used in France (pronounced *keress*) for that delightful apéritif, should you happen to want one in Paris.

Yeast

A microscopic organism that lives on grape skins (among other places) and is responsible for fermenting their juice into alcohol. (See also Fermentation.)

Yquem, Château d'

The only white wine, in fact the only wine, to be given the rank of *grand premier cru* outside the Médoc in the French classification of the great wines of Bordeaux in 1855. It is a Sauternes, and the estate has been in the same family for over 200 years. It takes one whole vine to make a single glass of Château d'Yquem. It is probably one of the most expensive wines in the world but it will keep for up to 100 years. You could buy a bottle and store it just to impress your friends, or to astonish your descendants.

Yugoslavia

The world's tenth largest producer of wine, a good deal of which is of very good value. Best known is its white Lutomer Laski Riesling (Laski being the Yugoslav name for the Wälschriesling grape), from Slovenia. Slovenia also makes Lutomer Sauvignon, which is also dry, Sylvaner (slightly sweet) and Traminer (fruity and fairly sweet). These are the country's most exported wines. The area has been making wine since the days of the Greeks and before.

A second important Yugoslav wine region is Dalmatia on

the Adriatic. Heavy, full-bodied tannic reds make up two-thirds of its output. From farther south in Macedonia, near the attractive, minaret-filled city of Mostar, comes one of the country's best white wines, Zilavka (see below) and a powerful red, Blatina (which means 'muddy'). Both are aromatic and alcoholic.

Serbia is Yugoslavia's most prolific wine producer, mainly of gutsy, rugged wines consumed locally.

Yugoslavia makes some 6.5 million hectolitres (149 million gallons) of wine a year. Most of it is blended, but the production of varietals is growing in response to demand.

Zilavka

Zilavka wine from what is now Yugoslavia was one of the favourites of the Austro-Hungarian emperors. Despite communism, there is still an 'Emperor's Vineyard' of Zilavka near Mostar. The word *zilavka*, inappropriately enough, means 'tough'.

Zinfandel

Wine from the red wine grape of the same name, a mysterious variety that California claims as its very own exclusive – its origins are lost in history. It is thought that it might have been imported into the USA by the Hungarian Agoston Haraszthy, who worked so hard to develop the Californian wine industry about 100 years ago. It might have been from his native land, but recent investigation seems to have decided that it could have originated as a grape from Bari in Italy.

Zinfandel is made into a very good red wine in California, where it is widely used. It has a fruity bouquet and a blackberry flavour (more or less). Best drunk young.

Index

126